The world at her fingertips

the story of helen keller

joan dash

Scholastic Press
NEW YORK

LIBRARY OF CONGRESS CATALOGING-IN-PUBLICATION DATA
Dash, Joan. The world at her fingertips: the story of Helen Keller / by Joan Dash. p. cm.
Includes bibliographical references and index.
ISBN: 0-590-90715-8
1. Keller, Helen, 1880–1968 — Juvenile literature. 2. Blind-deaf woman — United States — Biography — Juvenile literature. 3. Blind-deaf — United States — Biography —Juvenile literature. 4. Sullivan, Annie, 1866–1916 — Juvenile literature. 5. Sullivan, Annie, 1866–1936 [1. Keller, Helen, 1880–1968. 2. Blind. 3. Deaf. 4. Physically handicapped. 5. Women — Biography.] I. Title. HV1624 K4 D35 2001   362.4'1'092 — dc21 [B] 00-034502

12 11 10 9 8 7 6 5 4 3   01 02 03 04
Printed in the United States of America   37
First edition, February 2001

The display type was set in Linoscript and XB Folio Extra Bold.
The text type was set in 12-point Weiss. Book design by Marijka Kostiw

{table of contents}

{one}

TUSCUMBIA

Helen Keller was born in June of 1880, in Tuscumbia, Alabama, a small, sleepy, very southern town. In her own words, "The beginning of my life was simple and much like every other little life. I came, I saw, I conquered, as the first baby in the family always does." But at the age of nineteen months she came down with a raging fever, and what was called acute congestion of the stomach and brain, and after that no part of her life would ever be simple again.

The doctor had said she might not recover, yet early one morning the fever left as suddenly as it came. She fell into a peaceful sleep. Waking from time to time, she saw light and dark, with the light growing dimmer day by day until there was only dark. Her mother, Kate, was giving Helen a bath when she happened to pass a hand in front of the baby's eyes, and it seemed to her that the eyes never blinked. She did it again, and again there was no response, no movement of the eyelids. No matter how many times she tried it was always the same. She understood that her little girl was blind.

They took her by train to a doctor in Union City, Tennessee, a long journey during which Helen shrieked without stopping. When they got there the doctor said there was nothing to be done for her eyes. Soon her parents learned the child was deaf as well. One evening, when the bell was rung for dinner, they noticed that she made no move to go, so they rattled a tin can filled with stones, that had once been one of her favorite toys. She never turned her head. They spoke to her gently, they yelled, but nothing changed.

She had learned to speak quite early, using a handful of words that strangers might not have recognized as words, but when she stopped hearing human speech, she stopped trying to speak, although not all at once. It happened slowly, over time. The last word she remembered was "water," and she went on making some sound for it after all other words were gone.

Once her strength returned, Helen was as healthy, alert, and energetic as she used to be. She had no way of knowing that the rest of the family saw and heard and spoke, or that she was in any way different from them, and she began doing what every child does. She explored her world, poking her fingers into anything they met, touching, tasting, sniffing, pinching. By following with her hands the movements and operations of other hands, she learned what those other hands were up to and began to imitate them.

The family that surrounded her tried to carry on with ordinary life as if this enormous tragedy had never fallen on them. What else could they do? It was a sizable family. The father, Arthur Keller, had been a captain in the Confederate Army; Helen's cousin Leila described him as "a splendid man, large and fine looking and a genuine Christian." Twenty years older than Kate, a widower when they married, he had two sons: James, who was about the same age as Kate, and William, a teenager the family called by his middle name, Simpson.

The sons addressed their father as "Captain," and so did everyone else. He was the editor and publisher of a weekly newspaper. Like many upper-middle-class Southerners in the years after the Civil War, he owned parcels of land here and there, as well as the family home, but he was always short of money. He was a devoted father, although often a wrong-headed one.

Kate Adams Keller, the Captain's young second wife, had a large southern household to run, which meant curing hams, putting up jellies and preserves, looking after the poultry, the vegetable garden, the old-fashioned flower garden, and supervising the black servants who lived in the same shacks they had occupied fifteen years earlier when they were slaves. Kate worked alongside them from early morning until after dinner. She was reserved in nature, thoughtful and inward-looking, and a great reader.

So there were the father and mother, the two big sons, the little girl who was locked inside her own body, and Eveline Keller, the Captain's older sister, known as Aunt Ev. Their home was about a mile out of town. In addition to the main house, Ivy Green, there were barns, stables, chicken coops, outhouses, a smokehouse, the servants' shacks, and a garden cottage. None of it was grand; even in Ivy Green none of the rooms was large or generous. It was a working farm in a rural backwater; if there was a single school for the blind anywhere in Alabama, Kate had never heard of it.

She went about her daily tasks and thought her private thoughts, with Helen going everywhere her mother went, clutching her skirts. Before the illness she had been a much-loved and loving child, and she still was. Her playmates had been Martha

Washington, the cook's little daughter, and Belle, an old hunting dog, and they were her playmates now. She bullied them just as she used to. And in her own way, she was still talkative.

She had learned to talk with signs; by the time Helen was five she had invented about fifty signs, some for people, some for things. A pull meant "come," a shove meant "go." When she wanted bread she acted out the cutting of slices and buttering them. Pinching a tiny bit of skin on her hand meant "small," spreading her fingers wide and bringing her hands together meant "large." If it was ice cream she wanted, she shivered, and made the motion of turning the handle of the ice-cream freezer.

She had a different sign for every member of the household, glasses for her father, a stroking motion against the cheek for her mother. She knew when company came because she felt the opening and shutting of the front door. When they left she waved her hand for good-bye, from a vague memory of what the gesture meant. She learned what keys were for, and one day locked her mother in the pantry when everyone else was out of earshot. Kate spent three hours pounding furiously on the pantry door, while Helen sat outside on the front steps, enjoying the vibrations of the pounding.

She was strong, active, reckless, and she was beginning to understand that other people talked with their lips. When she moved her own lips the same way, nothing happened. Sometimes this made her so angry that she kicked and screamed until she was exhausted.

It seemed to her that her self, her normal childhood self, was taken over at times by another self — a powerful being that she called "Phantom" when she wrote about it many years later: "Helplessly the family witnessed the baffled intelligence as Phantom's hands stretched out to feel the shapes which she could reach but which meant nothing to her." She struck out at this unknowable world, hitting, kicking, blazing up in outbursts of anger that grew more and more frequent.

Nobody knew how to calm the wild, destructive little animal she had become. She broke lamps, shattered dishes, stuck her fingers into everybody's plates when they were having their meals, and ate what she liked, roaming from plate to plate. In the opinion of her uncle Fred, Helen no longer belonged with the family. He told his sister, "You really ought to put that child away, Kate; she is mentally defective and it is not very pleasant to see her about." Aunt Ev had a different opinion. According to Aunt Ev, Helen had more sense than all the Kellers; it was only a question of finding some way to reach her mind.

Then Helen learned she was no longer her mother's only darling. There was a new baby, her sister Mildred. Held and rocked in her mother's arms, this newcomer occupied the place that used to be Helen's alone. One day she rushed at the baby's cradle, overturned it, and toppled the baby out — Kate caught her just in time. How did you reach a mind that was locked in silent darkness? Helen was growing bigger and stronger day by day, and wilier too. She got whatever she wanted by manipulating her elders. What would her future be? The thought of a twenty-year-old Helen roaming through Ivy Green, uttering those choked screams to express anger, sightless and speechless and shut out from all human companionship, must have been terrifying to Kate.

Helen was taken to another doctor. Although he could do nothing for her, he offered the first ray of hope. They must consult Alexander Graham Bell in Washington, D.C., he said — the same Dr. Bell who was world-famous for inventing the telephone. Dr. Bell would know about teachers of deaf or blind children.

So they went to Washington, the Captain, Aunt Ev, and Helen, leaving Kate at home with the baby. In preparation for the trip, Kate had curled her daughter's hair with a curling iron and brushed out the bangs that framed her face. It was a wonderfully pretty face, with delicate features and an unusual expression — a questioning look under raised eyebrows.

When she came before Dr. Bell, he lifted her onto his lap and gave her his watch to play with. He was a big man, heavily bearded. Later in life, Helen remembered the watch and the beard, and the sense she had of being surrounded by love when she sat on his lap.

What Bell remembered was that "in her well-shaped face, for all its intimations of dormant intelligence, there seemed to be an indefinable, chilling emptiness."

Although he was known for inventing the telephone, Dr. Bell's lifelong interest had always been the education of the deaf. His mother had been deaf, and so was his beautiful wife. Now he instructed the Captain to write to the Perkins Institution for the Blind in Boston, and tell the director the Kellers needed a teacher for a deaf-blind child. It was at the Perkins School, forty years earlier, Dr. Bell explained, that another deaf-blind child had been taught to read and write and to speak with hand gestures. She was still alive, still at Perkins. What was done for her could surely be done for the Captain's daughter.

The Kellers went home to Tuscumbia, and a letter was sent to Michael Anagnos, the director of the Perkins Institution. (After 1955, it was known as the Perkins School.) When he answered he said he had someone in mind. He had been discussing it with her. Could the Captain tell them how much he proposed to pay?

The teacher Anagnos had in mind was a recent graduate of Perkins — not blind, although she had been partially blind for many years. Her name was Anne Sullivan, Annie to everyone who knew her; she was twenty years old.

As Annie remembered it, when Mr. Anagnos asked if she thought she could teach this little girl, she was very sure she couldn't. She wasn't trained for it; she wasn't, in fact, trained for anything. One moment she told herself she was too good for work of that kind. It would amount to burying herself in a small southern town when she longed for excitement and novelty, when she was far too young to be buried alive. The next moment she reminded herself that she needed a job. Any job.

She was absolutely alone in the world. Her education had been brief and sketchy, her childhood was squalid. She had no choice, then. She would have to go to Tuscumbia.

two

TEWKSBURY

*I*n Massachusetts, the state poorhouse at Tewksbury was a huddle of shabby buildings housing about a thousand inmates, on each of whom the state spent $1.88 a week. In 1876 Annie Sullivan, aged ten, and her five-year-old brother, Jimmie, had been placed in a farmer's cart and delivered to the Tewksbury poorhouse because their relatives couldn't think of anything better to do with them.

To begin with, their parents had been penniless Irish immigrants, illiterate and unskilled. Now their mother was dead. Their father, a shiftless drunk with an explosive temper, was hardly able to care for himself, and nobody wanted Annie, who was half-blind from trachoma, or Jimmie, who had a tubercular hip and walked with a crutch. Neither of them had ever been to school.

When they arrived in Tewksbury, the children learned they would have to be separated — boys and men lived in one place, girls and women in another. Annie howled when she heard it, so loudly and desperately that they were allowed to stay together in the women's ward of the hospital. That first night, they slept in a single bed in what Annie remembered as a small, dark enclosure, perhaps ten feet long, at the end of the ward. It was the place where corpses were wheeled to await burial. People called it the "dead house."

From then on they were assigned to a bed apiece, side by side in the women's ward. One morning Jimmie developed a high fever. That night, while Annie slept, he died very quietly, so quietly that Annie never heard them roll his bed away. But when she awoke and found him gone she knew what had happened, and ran screaming into the dead house to clutch the bars of his iron bed, screaming until she had screamed the whole place awake. People tried to pull her off, but she kicked and scratched and bit, so they dropped her on the floor and left her there. She remembered wanting to die.

Meanwhile, the world outside was growing suspicious of Tewksbury. Infants who were born there died within months, people said. The place was so short of money they couldn't afford to separate the sane from the insane, or those with contagious diseases from everyone else, and rats were said to be everywhere. The children were even said to have played with the rats.

A committee was formed to investigate the poorhouse. Annie heard it would be headed by Mr. Frank Sanborn, chairman of the State Board of Charities. He was the powerful one, the one who could get her out of Tewksbury and into a school where she would learn to read.

When they came, Annie followed them as they moved through the building, wondering which was Mr. Sanborn. Every face looked blurry to her, but even if she could see them clearly, how could she tell who he was? As they were ready to leave she threw herself into their midst, crying, "Mr. Sanborn, Mr. Sanborn, I want to go to school!"

Someone asked what was wrong with her, and she mumbled, "I can't see very well."

They asked how long she had been in the poorhouse, and she said she didn't know. The committee left. Annie learned a little later that she was going to school after all — leaving Tewksbury, to be educated at the Perkins Institution in South Boston.

It was October 1880, and she was fourteen years

old, a good-looking, dark-haired girl, sturdily built. She had her father's temper, she had occasional black moods when the world seemed hateful to her, but she was also quick-witted, thoroughly down-to-earth, and tough. She would need those qualities at Perkins.

The school was a famous one, largely because of the man who founded it, Dr. Samuel Gridley Howe, and his pupil Laura Bridgman — the deaf-blind child he had taught to read, write, and speak with her fingers. Educators all over the world knew the story, and Boston was immensely proud of it.

The children who came to Perkins belonged to the best middle-class families. They were bright and well mannered and, for the most part, adjusted to their blindness. They were still children, however, and quick to take advantage of anyone they felt to be inferior. On her first day at Perkins Annie was brought to a singing class where the teacher, who was blind, asked for her name.

"Annie Sullivan."

"Spell it," the teacher said. But of course she couldn't, and the class of teenage girls burst out laughing.

"How old are you?" asked the teacher. She said she was fourteen. "Fourteen and can't spell?"

Horribly humiliated, Annie had to listen to more laughter; even the teacher laughed. She had to learn the alphabet, using the raised type Dr. Howe favored, then she learned spelling, reading, simple arithmetic, everything her classmates had known since they were six years old — a great gawk of a girl, starting from the beginning and mocked by everyone. Homesick for Tewksbury and lonelier than she had ever been, she cried herself to sleep every night.

But she refused to let it show. She pretended she didn't care, pretended to be scornful and contemptuous of the others. "When is your brain awake?" one teacher demanded. "When I leave your class," Annie shot back.

Michael Anagnos took notice of her and arranged for her to have two eye operations, a year apart, that gave her almost normal vision. She taught herself to read ordinary print, and began to enjoy some of her classes. Yet she was still a rebel, claiming to despise all middle-class people, which meant everyone who was not Irish, Catholic, and wretchedly poor.

One day Laura Bridgman came to the cottage where Annie lived. She was a thin, plain-looking woman of fifty, who sewed and made beautiful lace but had never learned to cope with the world outside; she continued to live at Perkins, spending a year in one of the residential cottages, then moving on to the next. When Laura lived in Annie's cottage, Annie learned the manual alphabet — words spelled out letter by letter into the "listener's" palm — in order to converse with her.

Graduation drew near. Out of four boys and four girls, it was Annie Sullivan who emerged as the top student, the one who delivered the commencement address. The others went home afterward, but Annie's only home was the Tewksbury poorhouse, where she wasn't wanted for the summer because part-time residents were discouraged. Fortunately for Annie she was invited by her housemother, Sophia Hopkins, to spend the summer at Cape Cod.

Captain Keller's first letter was forwarded to her there, and Annie wrote to Anagnos, asking if she might come back to Perkins and go over the records Dr. Howe had kept when he was Laura Bridgman's teacher. Anagnos encouraged her to do so, even though the job was not yet definitely offered. Annie returned and studied Dr. Howe's methods — which were entirely his own invention, at once straightforward and easy to understand.

There was another letter from the Captain, this time with a firm offer: room, board, laundry, and a salary of twenty-five dollars a month. She would be treated like a member of the family.

Twenty-five dollars every month, with all her other expenses paid? It seemed most generous to Annie. She told the Captain she accepted, and promised herself she would spend all her earnings on clothes, extravagant and beautiful clothes, that would be hers alone — not charity clothes or hand-me-downs.

Two months later, she set out by train for Tuscumbia, a journey of several days and nights. Because she was still unsure she had made the right decision, she cried a good deal, which irritated her right eye. Pain and anxiety kept her from sleeping; when she did sleep she was pursued by nightmares.

{three}

TEACHER ARRIVES

$\mathcal{I}$t was a late afternoon in March 1887, three months before Helen's seventh birthday, and the Kellers were expecting Annie Sullivan. For two days one or another of them had gone with Kate to the station, meeting every train because they didn't know which one Annie would be on.

Helen, too, was waiting. Standing on the sunny porch, she felt the repeated opening and shutting of doors and the vibration of many footsteps. She knew the family were tense and excited, and she wanted to find out why.

That evening Annie Sullivan — her eyes inflamed, her body quivering with anxiety — arrived on the six-thirty train. She rode back in the carriage with Kate and her stepson James. They went into the garden, where the Captain welcomed her, then they moved to the porch. Now Annie saw the child from close up, and saw that she was robust and strong. Dirty, perhaps troublesome, but certainly not spiritless, for the face was intelligent and eager.

What Helen remembered were approaching foot-steps, her own outstretched hand, and somebody taking it. She thought at first it was her mother, embracing her and wanting to kiss her, and when she found it was a stranger, she struggled frantically to break free. She explored the unknown face, the dress, the bag, which she grabbed and tried to open. It was hard to do. She felt carefully, searching for a keyhole, and when she found it she faced the stranger, made the sign for turning a key, and pointed to the bag, because there was surely something good to eat in it — visitors usually brought her treats, and she wanted them now, immediately.

Kate took the bag away. At this, the child's face grew red to the roots of her hair, as Annie wrote later to Mrs. Hopkins, and she clutched at her mother's dress while kicking violently.

Annie brought out her little watch and managed to hold it against Helen's face; once the child felt the ticking, the tempest subsided.

Next morning Helen was taken to Annie's room and allowed to help unpack her trunk, where she found a doll the little girls at Perkins had sent;

the doll's clothes were specially made by Laura Bridgman. Annie decided this was the moment to teach Helen her first word.

"I spelled *d-o-l-l* slowly in her hand and pointed to the doll and nodded my head, which seems to be her sign for possession," Annie wrote to Mrs. Hopkins. "Whenever anybody gives her anything, she points to it, then to herself, and nods her head. . . . I took the doll, meaning to give it back to her when she had made the letters; but she thought I meant to take it from her, and in an instant she was in a temper, and tried to seize the doll. I shook my head and tried to form the letters with her fingers; but she got more and more angry. I forced her into a chair and held her there until I was nearly exhausted."

It occurred to Annie then that it was useless to continue the struggle, and she let the child go, but without giving her the doll. Running downstairs, she got some cake, brought it to Helen, and spelled *c-a-k-e* into Helen's hand while holding the cake out to her. "Of course she wanted it and tried to take it; but I spelled the word again and patted her hand. She made the letters rapidly, and I gave her the cake, which she ate in a great hurry. . . . Then I showed her the doll

and spelled the word again. . . . She made the letters
d-o-l and I made the other *l* and gave her the doll."
Then Helen fled downstairs and refused to have anything to do with Annie for the rest of that day.

"The greatest problem I shall have to solve is how
to discipline and control her without breaking her
spirit," Annie wrote to Mrs. Hopkins.

The spelling lessons continued, alternating with
lessons in the stringing of kindergarten beads and the
sewing of sewing-cards, all brought from Perkins.
Helen did them well, and with pleasure, and there
were no more displays of temper for a while. But a few
days later Annie had a battle royal with Helen, and
this time it was a Helen she had not met before. This
time she saw the Helen who belonged to Phantom,
her tyrant self.

The family was in the dining room eating breakfast,
and Helen stuck her hand into one plate after another
to grab whatever she liked. Then she stuck her hand
into Annie's plate. The hand was removed and set
firmly aside. Bewildered, Helen tried again, and again
her hand was removed and set aside. Several times,
many times. There was mounting fear and anger on
Helen's part. The family suffered for her, longing to

see her eat, no matter how, but Annie would not allow it. Then one by one, the family quietly tiptoed out of the dining room.

Annie gave her a spoon. Phantom hurled it to the floor. Annie pried her out of her chair and compelled her to pick up the spoon, compelled her to take up food with it, then forced the food into her mouth. When this "breakfast" was finished, the two of them spent an hour locked in battle over the folding of Phantom's napkin, after which Annie opened the door, letting Helen out into the warm sunshine, then went up to her room to cry her heart out.

There would be more battles, often dangerous ones for Annie. Because of the bottled-up rage within her, the child possessed exceptional strength — and yet she wasn't aware of it, in the sense of knowing cause and effect. She had no way of connecting the kicks and blows she aimed at this unknown Someone with the Someone who was hurt by them. Phantom knew nothing about other people's feelings, or about other people. Phantom was a stranger to love, to reason, to everything but instinct.

Once Helen refused to sit down at a table to learn any more of this finger business, and emphasized her refusal by kicking over the table. Annie set the table back in place, and insisted they go on with the lesson. Then Helen's fist flew like lightning and knocked out one of Annie's front teeth. Phantom again: Phantom making her presence felt. Helen's parents were, of course, aware of Helen's tyranny when she was under the spell of Phantom. They, too, had suffered from it, had been black and blue at times from her flat refusal to do anything except what she wanted to do. Yet they always rushed to protect their poor afflicted child.

Annie knew it was not protection she needed, not even love, not yet. She needed to be taken away from the family, out of their sight and hearing, beyond the reach of their protection. It was a great deal to ask of the Kellers, but Annie did ask, and eventually they agreed.

Soon Helen found herself in a place that was strange to her, where she felt lost, abandoned. She remembered one particular morning when she and the stranger began some kind of scuffling, going around and around an object that was probably a bed. The stranger showed her by firm movements that she must either lie down on the bed, or else get up and dress. She refused to do either. She behaved like a wild horse, Helen said later, because she was caged in this unknown place, with an unknown person larger and stronger than she was.

But it was only the garden cottage, with all the furniture changed, the door kept locked, and their meals sent in to them. If Helen had known she was a stone's throw from Ivy Green, she would have fled to her parents, but she couldn't know — they had taken her there by a roundabout route, without warning or explanation. Another thing she had no way of knowing was that her father stopped by every morning to look through the window.

Once he saw Helen still in her nightgown, sitting on the floor, her breakfast untouched on the table; it seemed to him she was the picture of despair. With tear-filled eyes, he went to Cousin Leila and told her, "I have a great mind to send that Yankee girl back to Boston. It is ten o'clock and poor little Helen has not been allowed to have breakfast." Aunt Ev, who happened to be present, told him, "No, Arthur, you must not feel that way. Miss Annie is going to be Helen's salvation."

In the garden cottage, Helen refused to let Annie near her. She went repeatedly to the door as if expecting someone, and from time to time she touched her cheek, which was her sign for her mother, then shook her head sadly. The lessons continued. As Annie told Mrs. Hopkins, "She has learned three new words, and when I give her the objects, the names of which she has learned, she spells them unhesitatingly." She was calmer, too. Or else resigned. "The little savage has learned her first lesson in obedience," Annie wrote.

Then word came that the Captain wanted them home. This was a disappointment to Annie, who had hoped the family would allow a longer stay. But they didn't or perhaps couldn't. A few weeks after they left Ivy Green for the cottage, teacher and pupil were back home with the others.

Annie established a routine. They spent early mornings outdoors, then came in for sewing, bead-stringing, and crocheting, all of which Helen enjoyed, although Annie considered them a waste of time. They went outdoors again for gymnastics, which was followed by an hour devoted to the learning of new words. By the end of the month Helen knew eighteen nouns and three verbs.

But Phantom was not yet defeated. According to Helen, "Phantom began to improve, but she still lacked the normal child's love of praise. She was not aware that she had been punished because she did not distinguish between right and wrong." She had no words for right and wrong. Although she was willing by now to repeat whatever finger-plays Annie put into the palm of her hand, she had no words. Like a clever dog, she had simply learned some tricks.

One morning — the morning when everything changed — they had a struggle over the words m-u-g and w-a-t-e-r. Annie tried to impress on Helen that m-u-g was mug and nothing else, and that w-a-t-e-r was water and nothing else, but Helen kept confusing the two. Annie gave it up for the time being.

Later, when Helen was playing with her new doll, Annie put an old rag doll into her lap, and spelled d-o-l-l, trying to show that the same word applied to both. Helen had had enough of this spelling. Seizing the new doll, she dashed it to the floor and felt a thrill of triumph when she felt the fragments at her feet.

They went outside, into the warm sunshine that Helen loved, then down the path to the well-house, where someone was drawing water. Annie put Helen's hand under the spout. Cool water gushed over that hand, as Annie spelled into the other hand the word w-a-t-e-r — first slowly, then rapidly.

Helen was startled for a moment. Then she stood very still, her whole being fixed on the two hands. Something stirred inside her. It seemed to her later that "somehow the mystery of language was revealed to me. I knew then that w-a-t-e-r meant the wonderful cool something that was flowing over my hand."

Everything had a name, the name and the thing were closely connected. "Suddenly I felt a misty consciousness as of something remembered — a thrill of returning thought." Flinging herself to the ground, she asked Annie for the name of what she was lying on. She pointed to the pump and wanted its name. Then the trellis. When she asked for the stranger's name, the stranger told her, "Teacher."

On the way back to the house Helen touched everything she could reach, and felt its name spelled letter by letter into her hand; as soon as a thing had a name, it began trembling with life. When she fell asleep that night, she could hardly wait for morning.

It was April now. A month had passed since Annie came to the Kellers, and the Captain paid her first month's salary. She wrote immediately to Michael Anagnos, saying she was ready to pay back what he had lent her for train fare. He refused to take it, urging her to start a savings account first, and repay him later. In the meanwhile, "I need scarcely say that I am deeply interested in your little pupil. She certainly is a re-markable child. . . . I have no doubt that ere long she will be able to talk."

Able to talk? Not only to talk with her fingers, but to do so "ere long"? Annie had already seen a clipping from the *Boston Herald*, an article that said Helen was "talking fluently." Michael Anagnos was surely respon-sible for it.

"Why, one might just as well say that a two-year-old child converses fluently when he says 'apple give,' or 'baby walk go,'" Annie told Mrs. Hopkins. She dis-liked this theatrical exaggeration, and for her pupil's sake was afraid of it. But there was nothing Annie could do to stop public fascination with Helen.

{ four }

FINGER-TALK

*H*elen had a little cousin, aged fifteen months. Whenever they went to visit her, Annie watched and listened. She saw that the baby understood a great deal — people told her, "Come," "Kiss," "Go to Papa," or "Shut the door," and she did as she was told. But while she understood the words, she never tried to say them.

Annie came to an interesting conclusion. The child had been born with the ability to learn language, and she couldn't help learning it, any more than a bird could help learning to fly. It was as if language had been built into her brain. She heard people talk, and at the right age she began to understand them; at another right age, she would imitate their talk.

Annie decided to use the same system with Helen. She would talk into Helen's hand the way people talked into the baby's ears — using complete sentences from the start, filling out the meaning with gestures. And all along she would do everything in her power to interest and stimulate Helen's mind. It was a method she thought up by herself; it had nothing to do with Dr. Howe, or Laura Bridgman, or anything found in books, but was solely the creation of twenty-year-old Annie Sullivan.

One day Annie walked into the room laughing. She put Helen's hand on her face, while spelling *laugh* into the other hand, then tickled Helen into a burst of laughter. Helen had not laughed since she lost her hearing, now she was gently persuaded into laughter. Annie took her through the motions of swinging, tumbling, jumping, hopping, skipping, each time suiting the spelled word to the act, and whenever she gave Helen a new word, Helen threw her arms around her teacher and hugged her.

By the end of April Helen knew more than a hundred words. A month later, almost three hundred. By June, four hundred, including mattress, bedstead, sheet, dust, and maple sugar.

And all this time Annie used no schedule, no schoolroom, no planned lessons. Helen was learning the way the baby learned — by being surrounded with spoken words. They set up a little store, filled it with provisions, and sold them for real coins that Helen touched and learned to tell apart. They went fishing with hooks and lines, and Helen caught a "very small fish," which was cooked for her supper. She held frogs in her hand to feel the throbbing throat. She dug bare-handed in the garden because Annie believed it was every child's natural-born right to dig in dirt. And whatever Helen was doing, her teacher described it for her in finger-talk while she was doing it.

During those months of spring, while Helen learned the names of things, another sort of learning took place. It had to do with the feelings that bound teacher to pupil. Helen had refused, at first, to let Annie kiss her; in those days she didn't want to be kissed by anyone but her mother. This changed after the day at the well-house, when Teacher threw open the door of the prison cell. From then on Helen kissed and embraced her teacher and learned to love her with a whole heart.

They were together all day long, and in the evenings, while Helen slept, Annie sat in their bedroom, holding one of Helen's dolls and singing to it. She had played with dolls all her life. Now, at the age of twenty, she had a real child to care for, one who was bright and strong and beautiful. "I feel in my heart that I belong to Helen, and it awes me when I think of it — this giving of one's life that another may live," she told

Mrs. Hopkins. "God help me to make the gift worthwhile!"

The word lessons continued. Once, when Helen was stringing the kindergarten beads — arranging different sizes in groups of two large, three small, and so forth — she made several mistakes that Annie pointed out. Then Helen discovered an error by herself; something was obviously wrong in the sequence of beads, but she couldn't tell what it was. Annie touched the child's forehead, at the same time spelling into her hand the word *Think*.

When Helen saw that this word was the name of the process going on in her head, it was her first understanding of an abstract idea.

She was learning adjectives and adverbs, and they came to her as easily as nouns. She was also discovering what the ordinary conversation of ordinary people was like — a difficult business for the deaf, to say nothing of the deaf-blind. Whenever they were with the family, Annie repeated to Helen everything that was said, and not just the bare bones, but the whole of it, complete with idioms, all translated into quick movements in the palm of the hand. The manual language is less mysterious than it seems. Kate had learned it within weeks of Annie's arrival, and the Captain learned the rudiments.

Helen was seven years old now, the age when most children are taught to read and write. And even though she had learned to speak less than three months earlier, in Annie's opinion she was as ready for books as any sighted child. This is how Helen remembered it: "As soon as I could spell a few words my teacher gave me slips of cardboard on which were printed words in raised letters. . . . I had a frame in which I could arrange the words in little sentences; but before I ever put sentences in the frame I used to [place them on] objects. I found the slips of paper which represented, for example, *doll*, *is*, *on*, *bed* and placed each name on its object; then I put my doll on the bed with the words *is*, *on*, *bed*, arranged beside the doll, thus making a sentence of the words with the things themselves."

One day she pinned the word *girl* on her dress; on a shelf she arranged the words *is*, *in*, *wardrobe*. Then she stood inside the wardrobe, waiting excitedly for her teacher to come and continue the game. The two of them played it for hours on end, sometimes with everything in the room arranged in sentences. A bystander might have had trouble deciding which one enjoyed it more.

They went on to the business of writing, using a wooden writing board that had grooves on it, a traditional tool for teaching writing to the blind. A paper was fitted over the board, then Helen formed the letters in the grooves, guiding her pencil with the forefinger of her left hand. This stiff-looking, angular script was known as "square hand."

Annie put one of the writing boards between folds of paper on the table and guided her pupil's fingers to form the sentence, "Cat does drink milk." Helen was delighted. She was writing. She could say whatever she liked in this square hand script. Soon she would be able to write letters, which was something grown-ups did. She could take the letters to the post office herself, and mail them herself.

Very soon after that she began learning Braille, the system of writing for the blind that uses characters made of raised dots; it was invented in 1824 by Louis Braille, a Frenchman who had been blind since early childhood. At the same time, Helen was making good progress in arithmetic. And then, without warning, she slipped backward into the embrace of Phantom, her savage self. The child of one of the servants, a girl named Viney, found Helen putting little stones into a glass tumbler, and thought she might break the glass. When Viney reached for the glass, Helen resisted. Viney tried to force it from her. Helen shrieked. Kicking, biting, and scratching at Viney, still shrieking and sobbing between shrieks, she began to shake all over.

Annie ran downstairs and grasped Helen's hand. She tap-tapped into it, wanting to know what had happened. Helen spelled: "Viney — bad," and renewed her attack on Viney. Annie held both her hands in a firm grip until at last she calmed down.

Later that day, Helen went to Annie and tried to kiss her, but Annie said, "I cannot kiss naughty girl."

"Helen is good, Viney is bad."

"You struck Viney and kicked her. . . . I cannot kiss naughty girl."

Helen stood very still for a moment, struggling with Phantom, then she tapped into Annie's hand, "Helen does not love Teacher. Helen do love Mother. Mother will whip Viney."

At dinner, Helen found that Annie wasn't eating. Her not eating was hurtful — why wasn't she eating? Annie said she couldn't eat because her heart was sad, and Helen began to cry and sob and cling to her. Yes, she would go with Annie while Annie told Viney that Helen was sorry. She would let Viney kiss her. But she wouldn't kiss Viney in return.

Although the incident ended well, it left Annie somewhat shaken. She told Mrs. Hopkins, "I had hoped this would never happen again." Helen had been so gentle and obedient the past two months that Annie thought love had subdued the lion, but it seemed he was only sleeping.

Annie, of course, had her own temper to deal with, her own sleeping lion. Now that the Captain could say a few words to Helen, he tended to forget he wasn't supposed to interfere with Annie's methods. From time to time he taught Helen one word or another, or sent for her in the middle of a lesson. This was galling to Annie, who resented any challenge to her authority over Helen's education.

She was also finding it hard to fit herself into a town so narrow and backward it seemed to belong to another century. Tuscumbia's population of three thousand consisted of blacks and whites in equal numbers, the blacks illiterate, living in ugly poverty and treated, in Annie's opinion, like household pets — indulged when they behaved, punished with pitiless severity when they failed to. At times it was amazing to her that she was employed by a family of former slave owners.

She missed Boston and big-city life, and never learned to love the South, but she made her peace with it for Helen's sake. Not only because she loved Helen, but because of another of her insights. In a long letter to Mrs. Hopkins, she wrote: "Something within me tells me that I shall succeed beyond my dreams. . . . I know that [Helen] has remarkable powers, and I believe that I shall be able to develop and mold them. I cannot tell how I know these things. I had no idea a short time ago how to go to work; I was feeling about in the dark; but somehow I know now, and I know that I know."

Anagnos asked Annie to write a paper about Helen for the school's annual report. While she worked on it, Helen sat beside her composing a letter for the little girls at Perkins: "papa does shoot ducks with gun and ducks fall in water . . . Helen does ride on horseback with teacher Helen does give hardee [her horse] grass in hand teacher does whip hardee to go fast Helen is tired Helen will put letter in envelope for blind girls."

Anagnos was charmed by the letter, and for Annie's composition he had only enraptured praise. Both were printed in their entirety in the annual report, complete with a picture of Annie and Helen, and several of Helen's letters.

The report was gobbled up by newspapers in the Boston area, who magnified it. Then it was picked up by other newspapers, and they magnified it yet again. Before long it had snowballed into a story of such out-size proportions, that some people, especially in Europe, perceived it as one more American claim to own whatever was biggest and best. Furthermore, there were teachers of the deaf-blind who suspected this Miss Sullivan of lying. How could anyone know what the child actually said, when everything had to be translated from the manual language by her teacher?

Yet there were many who believed in the miracle, including Alexander Graham Bell, an expert on the education of the deaf. Between the doubters and the believers, Helen was well on her way to becoming one of the most famous children in the world.

As Christmas approached, Annie and Helen prepared for it by reading books about Christmas, making up their own Christmas stories, and in general exploring the possibilities of Christmas — for it was Helen's first. Before, she had never understood what was going on around her during the holiday season, and never took part in it. Now, with Annie's help, she prepared surprises for everyone, and hugged the secrets to herself, thrilled by the game of hints and half-spelled sentences. "The mystery that surrounded the gifts was my greatest delight and amusement," she recalled.

Everyone in the family was deeply moved by the difference between this bright Christmas and all the others, when the child was held prisoner by Phantom, locked in the world that was a "no-world," as Helen described it later. Once Kate said, with tears in her eyes, "Miss Annie, I thank God every day of my life for sending you to us; but I never realized until this morning what a blessing you have been to us." Captain Keller took her hand, and could not speak, but to Annie his silence was more eloquent than words. Her own heart was full of gratitude and solemn joy.

The new year started. Helen would be eight that year, and would embark upon her first great adventure, a visit to Boston. The year would also bring the beginning of the end of Helen's life with her family. She would always love them, she would come back to them repeatedly, but she would never again belong to them the way Mildred did, or her brother, Phillips Brooks, who was born a few years later.

{ five }

BOSTON

*I*nstead of going directly to the Perkins Institution, Annie and Helen stopped first in Washington, D.C., where they had been invited to meet President Grover Cleveland. As Helen described the visit, "He lives in a very large and beautiful white house, and there are lovely flowers and many trees. . . . Mr. Cleveland was very glad to see me."

Then they set out for Boston and the school, arriving on May 26, 1888. Helen met the blind children, she played with them, talked finger-talk with them, kissed them, did beadwork and knitting with them, explored their embossed maps and the typewriter especially designed for the blind. Then Annie took her to visit Laura Bridgman.

They found her sitting by a window in her room, crocheting lace; when Annie put her hand on Laura's hand, there was instant recognition. And then, as Helen recalled, "She kissed me kindly, but when I tried to examine the lace, she instinctively put it out of my reach, spelling rather emphatically, 'I'm afraid your hands are not clean.'"

Helen wanted to touch Laura's face, but "she shrank away like a mimosa blossom from my peering fingers. . . . Laura was extremely dainty in all her ways, and exquisitely neat. My strong, impulsive movements disturbed her greatly." Helen started to sit on the floor, but Laura pulled her up, spelling, "You must not sit on the floor when you have on a clean dress." When they were ready to leave, Helen tried to kiss Laura goodbye, and in the process stepped on her toes, which made Laura so thoroughly annoyed that Helen felt like the bad little girl of the Sunday-school books.

There were people at Perkins who found Helen too much of a tomboy, too eager to put herself forward. Such a contrast with gentle, ladylike Laura, they said. They held Annie Sullivan to blame, and to some degree they were right, since she was the one who taught Helen to laugh out loud, to climb trees, and dig barehanded in the dirt. Annie must have been very much aware of the contrast between the two, when she first brought Helen to Laura Bridgman, sitting in the quiet room where she made her lace.

The next event in their Boston visit was the Perkins commencement, a grand occasion that always drew overflow crowds. The governor of Massachusetts sat on the platform, face to face with the cream of Boston society and representatives of the great colleges for which the city was famous. The Perkins students sang, their brass band performed, ten little boys were examined in mental arithmetic, and then Helen appeared.

Standing with Annie at a table, her face glowing with anticipation, she sensed the audience — their movements, their perfumes and odors, and the scraping of their chairs. When the moment came for her to perform, her whole body seemed to tremble. With the fingers of her left hand she read a poem about birds, spelling it into Annie's palm with the other hand. Annie recited the words aloud. The audience was enthralled.

After the ceremony, many of the guests stayed behind to watch Helen, some waiting to speak to her with Annie's help. There was something about the child that attracted others. She was so radiantly alive, so eager to embrace people when she met them, old or young, male or female, although Annie suspected a preference for men and boys. In a letter to her mother a few months later, Helen described a reunion with the children of some family friends: "Clifton did not kiss me because he does not like to kiss little girls. He is shy. I am very glad that Frank and Clarence and Robbie and Eddie and Charles and George were not very shy."

When Perkins closed for the summer, Helen and Annie went home with Mrs. Hopkins to Cape Cod. For Helen, who had read about the ocean but had never been near it, this was her first opportunity to "touch the mighty sea and feel it roar."

No sooner was she helped into her bathing suit, than she sprang out onto the sand and plunged into the water. "I felt the great billows rock and sink. The buoyant motion of the water filled me with an exquisite, quivering joy," she remembered. "Suddenly my ecstasy gave place to terror; for my foot struck against a rock and the next instant there was a rush of water over my head." She stuck out her hands, searching for support. She grabbed at seaweed, at water. Adrift and terrified, gasping for breath, she was hurled back onshore without warning, and in an instant folded in her teacher's arms. As soon as she recovered from her first panic, she demanded: "Who put salt in water?" The wonder of it was that only a few days later her courage returned and she was back in the water once more, being thrown around by waves.

Then they were home again in Tuscumbia, taking long walks to a place called Keller's Landing. It was an old lumber wharf on the Tennessee River, where Helen learned geography by making miniature islands and lakes, digging riverbeds, and building dams of pebbles. Annie told her about "the great round world with its burning mountains, buried cities, moving rivers of ice." They studied longitude and latitude, using strings, with sticks for the poles. They turned Helen's room into a wigwam, a castle, a fort, a Greek marketplace; they fought the American Revolution and acted out myths, and everything Helen learned seemed more like play than learning.

But Annie was no happier in Tuscumbia than she used to be. It was a horrid little town, she said. People snubbed her. She felt caged, in exile. Helen, too, missed Boston; she told her father to earn a great deal of money and buy a big house there. But she was not miserable, in exile, or caged, and she spent much of her time writing to the many friends she had made in the East.

Annie, bristling: "But most of those letters are written to strangers and not to your friends."

"They are my friends because they think of me and write to me," Helen said.

Annie did not intend to remain in exile for long. She told the Kellers that Helen deserved to be at Perkins. The child had such an appetite for learning. She needed to know everything, to understand everything. At Perkins there was systematic and specialized teaching, a large library for the blind, and at their doorstep one of the nation's finest, most historic cities.

Reluctantly, the Kellers agreed, and arrangements were made for Helen and Annie to come to Perkins as guests of the school. They arrived in October, and Helen plunged in directly — geography, botany, zoology, arithmetic. At dinner, she went up to one of the teachers, Fanny Marrett, and said, "Will you teach me French?" Miss Marrett would, and did, and was amazed by Helen's memory. When beginning the second lesson, Miss Marrett was ready to review the words from the first lesson — but Helen said, in an emphatic, surprised way, "I know them! Please teach me something new!"

Not only was she hungry for information, she insisted on digesting and mastering it. Once, when puzzled by some problem in her homework, she told Annie about it; Annie suggested the two of them go for a walk, and then perhaps understanding would come. But Helen refused to run away from her difficulties. "I must stay and conquer them now," she said.

She was passionately fond of poetry. After reading some works by John Greenleaf Whittier, she wrote to thank him for his beautiful poems — "I love you very dearly," she told him. She was taken to visit Oliver Wendell Holmes, the great New England writer, and sent him a letter afterward; Holmes published it in a column he contributed to *Atlantic Monthly* magazine. She composed little stories. She wrote a letter to *St. Nicholas*, the periodical for children, and it was printed there.

In the spring of 1890, Mary Swift Lamson, who had been one of Laura Bridgman's teachers, returned to the school after visiting Norway. She told Annie and Helen about a Norwegian girl, Ragnhild Kaata, who was deaf and blind and who had been taught to speak aloud. Mrs. Lamson had scarcely finished before Helen was on fire with eagerness. She resolved that she too would learn to speak.

Annie discouraged it. She said the voices of deaf children sounded unpleasant to her. But Helen gave her no peace, for the possibility of speech had been on her mind a long time. In their first days at Perkins she had asked her teacher, "How do the blind girls know what to say with their mouths? Why do you not teach me to talk like them? Do deaf children ever learn to speak?"

Annie had explained at the time that some deaf children did learn to speak, but they had the advantage of being able to see their teachers' mouths, and this guided them.

Helen never gave up the dream. As soon as she heard about the Norwegian girl, there was no restraining her — she must and would be taught to speak. Annie surrendered. They went together to the Horace Mann School for the Deaf in Boston, whose principal was Sarah Fuller, a woman greatly admired by Dr. Bell.

Miss Fuller offered to teach the child herself, beginning then and there. Taking one of Helen's hands, she placed it on the lower part of her own face. Helen's other hand was put inside Miss Fuller's mouth, where she could feel how the tongue and lips were positioned. Then Miss Fuller made the sound of *i* as in *it*. By the end of that first lesson — there would be eleven altogether — Helen had learned to pronounce the letters *i, m, p, a, s, t*. In her mind's eye she saw herself returning to Tuscumbia and embracing the family one by one, while saying each of their names aloud — and then she would touch their faces to feel the expressions of joyful surprise. Her little sister would understand her now, Helen thought: "I used to repeat ecstatically, 'I am not dumb now.'"

In the times between lessons, she practiced constantly. One of Helen's Alabama cousins remembered Annie's role in those practice sessions. Her mouth would be open, wide enough so that Helen could put her fingers all the way in, sometimes far down into the throat. Annie might be nauseated, yet unless she managed at the same time to make the sound Helen was learning to copy, the point of the lesson would be lost.

While she practiced Helen was learning something else, a by-product of the speech lessons that would prove to be equally valuable: She was taught to read the speech of others with her fingers. By placing her middle finger on the nose, her forefinger on the lips, and her thumb on the throat of that other person, she could follow what was said. This lip-reading was probably the least publicized of Helen's accomplishments, but one of the most remarkable.

She discovered later that her speech was imperfect and sadly limited. But she spoke, in a living voice, and it was something she had wanted for herself — not what Annie wanted, what Helen wanted. It gave her a feeling of independence, something else she longed for. She was eleven years old now, halfway to being twelve and not far from the start of adolescence, and in many ways remarkably like other girls that age. She was also unlike them in many ways. She lived in a beautiful world inhabited only by kindhearted people who trusted and loved one another, and in this beautiful world everyone loved her.

Helen's belief in universal loving-kindness was about to be tested.

{ six }

THE FROST KING

*I*n 1891, Helen wrote a little story, "The Frost King," as a birthday present for Mr. Anagnos. The family read it and talked about it, as Annie recalled, and agreed it was a marvelous creation — so imaginative, so flooded with color. Yet it was hard to understand how Helen came to describe these colors without being able to see them. Where did you read this lovely story, they asked her. Helen told them, "I did not read it; it is my story for Mr. Anagnos's birthday." Then she carried it to the post office and mailed it.

The story was overly sweet and sentimental, although very much in keeping with some children's literature of the time. It had to do with a collection of precious stones belonging to the Frost King, who sent them to Santa Claus, after which they were magically used to paint the leaves of oak and maple trees. Anagnos, who found it captivating, sent it to *The Mentor*, a publication of the Perkins alumni association, where it appeared in January, 1892.

One morning toward the end of that month, Helen waited for Annie to come upstairs and comb out her hair. When Annie came she brought a thunderbolt. "Someone wrote to Mr. Anagnos," Helen told her diary, "that the story which I sent him as a birthday gift, and which I wrote myself, was not my story at all, but that a lady had written it a long time ago."

After its appearance in the Perkins publication, the story had been picked up by the *Goodson Gazette*, whose editors recalled something very similar that was written years earlier, a story called "The Frost Fairies" by Margaret Canby. Long sections of Helen's story were then published in the *Gazette*, side by side with sections from Mrs. Canby's work — and in places they were not only similar, but identical, paragraph for paragraph, word for word.

Helen went to bed that night confused and miserable. She had never heard Mrs. Canby's story, she said: "I do not know what I shall do. I never thought that people could make such mistakes. . . . Mr. Anagnos is much troubled. It grieves me to think that I have been the cause of his unhappiness. . . ."

The editors of the *Gazette* wanted it known that they did not blame "little Helen Keller for the attempt at fraud, far from it. . . . The blame for the fraud rests not upon her, but upon whoever knowingly attempted to palm off The Frost King as her composition and there the blame will be."

They meant Miss Sullivan. At Perkins and elsewhere in Boston, a good many people were eager to see Annie Sullivan as the villain in this drama. Mr. Anagnos was not one of them. He was genuinely proud of Annie, and he loved Helen. But everywhere he turned, he seemed to hear the word "plagiarism," as if the whole of Boston had seen those parallel columns. He had the school's reputation to think of, as well as his own, and he panicked.

He directed that every book in the library be searched for a copy of the Canby story. Every teacher must be examined to see if she remembered reading it to Helen, discussing it with Helen. Anxious inquiries were sent to the Kellers. But no trace of the story could be found, nobody had even heard of it.

Anagnos should have thrown up his hands at this point, should have said this was a mysterious business, one that might never be explained, but that it was also unimportant. Helen had sent him a birthday greeting. One that was never meant for publication. Why did it matter where this birthday greeting came from? Instead, he had Helen and Annie brought before an examining committee — all teachers or officers of the school, four of them blind, four sighted. Then Annie was instructed to go, leaving Helen at the mercy of the court.

She was questioned and cross-questioned by judges who seemed determined to make her admit that "The Frost Fairies" had been read to her. Doubt and suspicion colored their every word. "The blood pressed about my thumping heart, and I could scarcely speak. . . ," Helen said later. "Even the consciousness that it was only a dreadful mistake did not lessen my suffering. . . ."

At the end of the inquisition, the committee was evenly divided, four for conviction, four for acquittal. But then Anagnos cast his vote in favor of Helen, and there the verdict rested — acquittal by a hair's breadth. When Helen went to bed that night, "I imagined I should die before morning, and the thought comforted me. I think if this sorrow had come to me when I was older, it would have broken my spirit beyond repairing." Nobody held Helen responsible, however; it was always Annie they blamed, Annie who had warped an innocent mind.

Annie maintained that Mrs. Hopkins had read the

story to Helen in the summer of 1888 — a very long time ago, it was true, but then Helen had an extraordinary memory. Annie denied up and down that she herself had ever heard of "The Frost Fairies," much less read it to Helen, and this was all she had to say on the subject.

What really happened? The only conceivable explanation is that Annie did indeed read the story to Helen. She might have seen no harm in Helen's using parts of it in her own version; she might also have been ignorant of laws against plagiarism, if such a term can be used about a personal letter. And by the time Annie came to understand that it meant the stealing of someone else's words or ideas, she lacked the courage to back down.

Mrs. Canby wrote to Helen and Annie; her letters were wise, generous, and affectionate. Samuel Clemens, writing as Mark Twain, had this to say ten years later when he came to know Helen: "Oh, dear me, how unspeakably funny and owlishly idiotic and grotesque was that 'plagiarism' farce! As if there was much of anything in any human utterance, oral or written, *except* plagiarism!"

As for Anagnos, to Helen and Annie both he tried

to remain the loving friend he had always been. In time, his attitude would change, but that was later. For now, it seemed that Perkins had been dealt a near mortal blow — and survived. Everything, everybody, went on more or less as before.

At the end of May, Annie and Helen traveled south to Ivy Green and a summer of misery. They found the Captain so heavily in debt that he borrowed thirty-five dollars from Annie. Everything the Kellers owned was mortgaged. Meanwhile Helen was pale, listless, preoccupied with her own anxieties.

There were hours when she sat quite still, not speaking, taking no interest in anything, not even her books. Something was wrong with her world; it used to be full of people who loved her: President Cleveland; the great inventor Dr. Bell; the teachers at Perkins. All of them had loved her once, and she had loved everyone in the world. But the world had changed. She could no longer be sure of being loved. Maybe she could no longer be sure of anything.

Sleepless, tormented by the heat of a southern summer, she was ill off and on for weeks at a time. Suppose she never got better? Once she tapped into Annie's hand her fears that she might die in this uncertain new world. The affair of "The Frost King" left such a bitter aftertaste that when Helen wrote about it years later, she said, "Joy deserted my heart and for a long time I lived in doubt, anxiety and fear. . . . The thought of those dreadful days chills my heart."

But then the weather changed. The air turned crisp, invigorating, and Helen showed signs of improvement. She had been asked to write a sketch of her life for *Youth's Companion*, and started work on it, although the thought "that what I wrote might not be absolutely my own tormented me," as she recalled. "Sometimes, in the midst of a paragraph I was writing, I said to myself, 'Suppose it should be found that all this was written by someone long ago!' . . . I wrote timidly, fearfully, but resolutely. . . ."

Bit by bit the pieces were assembled into a whole and read to Annie, who was very much moved by them, and in mid-December Helen mailed off a completed manuscript. The editor was so delighted that he sent Helen a check for one hundred dollars. This was followed, in January, by a New Year's present of fifty dollars from that same editor who published the article in January 1894. A philanthropist in Philadelphia sent money; John Spaulding, another rich benefactor, gave

Helen fifteen shares of stock from a trust he had founded. Yet she was frequently sick during the holidays, and the generosity of her friends was further spoiled by her father's interference. He took charge of the stock, the money gifts, even the check for her article, which she had hoped to use to start a lending library in Tuscumbia. Now the money for such a project was out of her hands.

There was no talk of their going back to Perkins, although Anagnos continued to urge it, at least to Helen. He wrote to her as tenderly as before, he missed her sorely, was interested in everything she did — but he rarely wrote to Annie. The winter wore on, a restless one without direction and without much in the way of education. They had a lesson now and then, but nothing seeming to lead anywhere, and nothing mattered very much.

Then, unexpectedly, a reprieve came, one that promised excitement and a change of scene. Captain Keller decided to go to Washington in March, bringing Helen, Annie, and Mildred. They would be present at the second inauguration of President Cleveland, they would go on to Boston, and after that to Chicago for the World's Fair of 1893. Helen was beside herself with joy, and Annie began to hope that Anagnos would meet them in Washington, that they would be friends again.

He never came to Washington. When Helen and Annie arrived in Boston, they saw that the friendship with Anagnos was over. "It was after 1893," Helen wrote some years later, "after we had ceased to avail ourselves of the hospitality of the Perkins Institution that Mr. Anagnos proved untrue to the friendship between us. It was then that he . . . declared and continued to declare to one person and another his opinion that we were one or both guilty. Once at the Kindergarten for the Blind in the presence of several friends, one of whom reported the matter direct to us, he said, 'Helen Keller is a living lie.'"

By this he meant, as he explained to the friend, that Annie had taught Helen to deceive. "That was the wrong Mr. Anagnos did my teacher," Helen's letter continues. "That was the untruth he told of me." It was a sad end to the sad story of "The Frost King." And it was not the last time Annie's temperament — her high-handedness, her inability to admit a mistake — would disrupt lives and friendships.

They turned increasingly to Helen's first friend,

Alexander Graham Bell. He became the guide and protector Anagnos used to be, but a far wiser and more experienced one. Helen had loved him from the first moment they met, and he loved her in return, both for herself and for a quality in her that touched him to the depths. "I feel that in this child I have seen more of the Divine," he once said, "than has been manifest in anyone I ever met before." He had two daughters, Elsie and Daisy, who were about the same age as Helen; they too became her friends and admirers. But there were times, when all three were in their teens, that the daughters felt twinges of jealousy because of their father's devotion to Helen.

After Boston and what Helen remembered as a thrilling detour to Niagara Falls, they went on to Chicago, where they were joined by Dr. Bell. In Jackson Park, facing Lake Michigan, the fairgrounds sprawled over 686 acres, and cost twenty-eight million dollars. More than twenty million visitors came to see it. Helen Keller, an eager, animated thirteen-year-old, attracted attention wherever she went. A photo taken at the time shows her in profile, her head covered with short curls, her neck long and graceful, everything about her almost painfully lovely.

Helen Keller, age seven, pictured with a dog (*American Foundation for the Blind, Helen Keller Archives*)

Helen reading at the Perkins Institution, later known as the Perkins School for the Blind *(Perkins School for the Blind)*

Helen with Michael Anagnos, the director of the Perkins Institution *(Perkins School for the Blind)*

Helen graduated *cum laude* from Radcliffe on her twenty-fourth birthday.
(AFB)

Here, Helen Keller, Annie Sullivan, and Alexander Graham Bell simultaneously use three modes of communication: Helen reads Annie's lips, Annie and Dr. Bell talk, and Dr. Bell finger spells into Helen's hand. *(AFB)*

Helen Keller, Annie Sullivan Macy, and her husband, John Macy, pictured at their house in Wrentham, Massachusetts *(AFB)*

Helen and Annie pictured with Mark Twain and Lawrence Hutton, whose wife managed a fund to help support Helen, c. 1902 *(AFB)*

Helen riding a horse in Beverly Hills, California *(AFB)*

After Annie was taken ill, Polly Thomson became their assistant, secretary, and loyal friend. Here, Helen enjoys trying on a hat with Polly Thomson at her side, c. 1954. *(AFB)*

Taken in 1918, this photograph shows Helen Keller; her brother, Phillips Brooks Keller; and their mother, Kate Keller, in a scene from *Deliverance*, a movie about Helen's life. *(AFB)*

A poster advertising *Deliverance* (*Perkins School for the Blind*)

She had been given official permission to touch even the most delicate things, so "I took in the glories of the Fair with my fingers," she wrote. "It was a sort of tangible kaleidoscope. . . . Everything fascinated me."

One evening they went to the midway, where Helen found the bazaars of India and the lagoons of Venice. She boarded a Viking ship, rode on a new ride called a Ferris wheel, named after its inventor, and also on a camel, and explored the "streets of Cairo." Her letter to John Spaulding describing the fair was later published in the magazine, *Saint Nicholas*. Dr. Bell began encouraging her to think about a career as a writer.

They spent three memorable weeks at the fair, but then the reprieve was over and the real, earnest, workaday world awaited them. Since the part of Helen's life belonging to Perkins was finished, like it or not, a new chapter would have to begin. Where would it take them? Helen's most earnest desire was to continue her education in a school for normal girls. She discussed it with Dr. Bell, and he immediately agreed, for he had always believed that the deaf must not inhabit a separate world.

Annie, who had the same belief, mulled over the possibilities. No public school could be expected to teach a deaf-blind student, and private schooling had to be paid for. In her opinion the Captain's financial affairs were not going to improve; he had failed to pay her salary for months, and as it happened was never able to do so again. This meant he would be unable to pay for the education that Dr. Bell and Annie wanted for Helen, and Helen wanted for herself.

Then a pathway opened. Annie heard about two young men — Dr. Thomas Humason, and John Wright — who planned to start a secondary school in New York where deaf youngsters would be taught to speak. Wright and Humason believed their methods would improve Helen's voice, that she might even be taught to sing. And John Spaulding was eager to pay for it.

Now all the questions about Helen's future education, which school would take her and where it would lead, found an answer in New York. The Wright-Humason School, as Helen wrote to a friend, was "quite fashionable." She would study arithmetic, English literature, American history, French and German, as well as lip-reading and speech — a broad and interesting high-school curriculum.

In the autumn of 1894, Helen and Annie settled

into a new life at the new school, in a pleasant house close to Central Park. A *New York Times* reporter came there one evening to interview Helen, who was accompanied by Topsy, her cat. A discussion followed about how she came to choose the cat's name. "The most remarkable part of this conversation was that it was carried on entirely by word of mouth," the reporter said. Helen answered every question "in the ordinary way," and she listened by placing her fingers on the speaker's face, the speaker being Dr. Humason, who spoke slowly and distinctly.

She used three typewriters with great neatness and accuracy, the interview continued. One was for her journal-writing. She was most conscientious about writing a certain amount every day, and "if original ideas give out the young girl proceeds to pad most conscientiously."

The reporter found her altogether amazing. Having read other interviews of Helen Keller, full of "exalted sentiments and . . . beautiful language," he had formed a picture of a remote and highly spiritual young person, entirely out of tune with the everyday world. But the girl he saw before him was clever and quick, she smiled and laughed and showed "a great enjoyment of life under conditions which would seem to many persons unbearable."

Helen went with her class to see the Statue of Liberty, climbing the staircase to stand in the head that overlooked the comings and goings of ships in the harbor. Another time the class went to the Dog Show at Madison Square Garden. One day, Helen and Annie set off on an expedition of their own to the slums of the Lower East Side, where new immigrants lived. The streets were crowded with people whose clothing smelled of machine oil and sawdust and salted fish and poverty. Inside the tenement dwellings were windowless rooms teeming with rats and cockroaches, and that same sour smell of poverty. It was an experience Helen never forgot.

Her speech was slow to improve. "I wonder why it is so difficult and perplexing for a deaf child to learn to speak when it is so easy for other people," she wrote to a Boston friend. But she was learning all the same.

{seven}

NEW YORK

$\mathcal{I}$t was a Sunday afternoon at the home of Lawrence Hutton, a writer and collector of books. A number of prominent people had dropped in, including Mark Twain. He stood among a cluster of guests, all of them awaiting the arrival of Helen Keller and Annie Sullivan — the wonderful child, as he put it, "with her almost equally wonderful teacher" — as if they were the celebrities and he was one of the fortunate few invited to meet them.

When she arrived, the guests were presented to her one by one, then she sat on a sofa with Annie beside her and the novelist William Dean Howells on the other side. Twain watched Helen place her fingers on Howells' lips, as he told her a story of considerable length, "and you could see each detail of it pass into her mind and strike fire there and throw the flash of it into her face."

Then Annie put one of Helen's hands to her own lips and spoke against it the question, "'What is Mr. Clemens distinguished for?' Helen answered, in her crippled speech, 'For his humor.' I spoke up modestly and said, 'and for his wisdom.' Helen said the same words instantly — 'and for his wisdom.' I suppose it was mental telegraphy for there was no way for her to know what I had said."

Helen was fourteen years old and Mark Twain was sixty, but she felt completely at home with him. She touched his hair and his face, and on impulse took some violets she had been given and put them in his buttonhole. She kissed him when he said good-bye. "I think he is very handsome indeed," she told her mother. It was the start of a friendship that lasted until his death.

New York was not Helen's favorite place, however. There were too many people, and they were in too much of a hurry. She felt their rapid footsteps pounding past her on the pavement, old and young, men and women, each with a characteristic step, and all of them going too fast. Were they watching her? Could they tell how different she was? She felt she was always on view, compelled to smile no matter what, because she could never tell whose eyes were measuring her.

But the school was close to Central Park, which was uncrowded and smelled like the country; Helen took walks there every day with Annie. With her fellow students, she went bobsledding on snowy winter days, spilling out of the sled along with the others when it came to grief. She talked Annie into letting her take riding lessons, and every morning they set out together on horseback from Durland's Academy, near Columbus Circle, with Dr. Humason, an expert horseman.

Unlike Helen, Annie found nothing good in New York. People were pleasant to her — there was little of the snobbishness she saw in Boston — but all the same, she was terrified that they might find out who she was. Meaning, they might learn about Tewksbury. To Annie, Tewksbury was a guilty secret, one she could not share even with Helen. It was as if this beloved child would be injured or soiled by it. Annie talked freely enough to Helen about her early years; her brother, Jimmie, and the games they used to play, but more than thirty years passed before she spoke about the dead house and Tewksbury.

A more immediate concern was the question of Helen's future. She was not making the progress they had hoped for in speech, and her classwork at Wright-Humason was not preparing her for college. College was on both their minds now. It had been on Helen's mind for several years.

As a little girl, she had visited Wellesley and surprised her friends by the announcement, "Someday I shall go to college — but I shall go to Harvard!" When her friends asked her why not Wellesley, she said there were only girls there. "The thought of going to college took root in my heart and became an earnest desire, which impelled me to enter into competition for a degree with seeing and hearing girls," she said. There were no girls at Harvard, then or for more than half a century to come. But Harvard had a sister college, Radcliffe, whose standards were the same as Harvard's.

Annie had been mulling over these matters since the end of their first year in New York. They were partly through the second year now, and it was increasingly clear that before Helen could qualify for Radcliffe, she would have to attend some other secondary school, one with a stronger academic curriculum. Yet Annie felt at times that she could not endure the thought of one more school. Any school. Annie had, in fact, a deep-rooted distrust of the entire education system.

There were times when she wondered if she ought to find another teacher for Helen, someone more capable of helping her prepare for college. Helen would never have agreed to it, however — for Helen, there was nobody on earth more worthy of love and admiration than her teacher. Nevertheless, she was in her mid-teens now, and aware of a change in her relations with Annie. It was surely the same change that takes place between a mother and a teenage daughter, for Teacher had become in effect Helen's foster mother.

What the daughter saw now, or was beginning to see, suspect, and sense, was that this much-loved mother was a separate person from her foster child. She had a temperament entirely different from Helen's, more high-strung, more changeable. There were times when Helen felt alone and bewildered by some of Annie's peculiarities. There was a strangeness, she said; a "something too subtle for words was lacking in our relations to each other."

Annie had that streak of what Helen called "melancholy," meaning occasional bouts of black depression. When such a mood overwhelmed her, she would feel driven to escape from people, going to bed or taking long walks alone in the woods. If she was near water, she might hide for hours at a time under a boat on the shore. As soon as the mood lifted, she appeared to be her old self again. Quick to anger, she was also quick to forgive.

There is more to be said about this anger of Teacher's. In the years after Phantom was defeated, Helen held on to certain habits that Teacher was determined to conquer — "the habits that make children repulsive," as Helen put it. This particular child was a nail-biter; she would not give up her nail-biting until "one day there descended upon her a human whirlwind who boxed her ears and tied her hands behind her back, thus shutting off all means of communication."

It was the equivalent of taping shut the mouth of a normal child, since Helen could talk only with her hands at that time.

Annie demanded the best, and only the best, from Helen. She expected a star-quality performance every time. This expectation arose partly from love, partly because Annie was Annie — a magnificent teacher, yet a difficult and complex person. Helen was only now beginning to catch true glimpses of that person.

Meanwhile, they discussed Radcliffe — without any idea of what Radcliffe's attitude would be once

Helen was ready to apply for entrance. A number of colleges accepted women, but nowhere in the country was there another in which women were held to the same high standards as those at Harvard, using the same curriculum, with progress tested by exactly the same exams.

Annie went to Cambridge, the town just outside of Boston that was home to Harvard as well as Radcliffe. There she called on Arthur Gilman, the head of the Cambridge School for Young Ladies. Gilman had been one of the founders of Radcliffe, and the sole purpose of his school was to prepare students for entrance to Radcliffe. When Annie asked if he would accept Helen Keller as a student, he was startled, but willing to think it over.

At least the sticky problem of paying for this education was finally resolved. Under the leadership of Mrs. Lawrence Hutton, a fund was put together; several friends, including Dr. Bell, contributed to it, and Mrs. Hutton believed that with time it would grow large enough to support Helen and Teacher throughout their lives.

That summer, with the news of her father's death, Helen experienced her first great loss. Frantic with grief, her one desire was to get to her mother, but Kate telegraphed to say it was the season of contagious diseases and she must not come. Helen was inconsolable.

A month later, holding tight to Annie's hand, she set off to begin her education at the Cambridge School, for Mr. Gilman had been unable to resist the challenge of teaching Latin, Greek, and French to a girl who could not see him, could not hear him, and could speak to him only with difficulty.

eight

CAMBRIDGE

$\mathcal{H}$elen's daily schedule was not very different from everyone else's. She lived with Annie in Howells House, one of the Cambridge School dormitories. She made friends with her classmates, and some of them learned the manual language. She joined them in many of their games, even blindman's bluff. "I took long walks with them," she said, "we discussed our studies and read aloud the things that interested us," and it seemed to her that she was doing everything they did, that she was truly one of them.

This pleasant glow, this joy in living the way others lived, was bound to fade, for Helen faced obstacles that her classmates could not share. Books printed for the blind were hard to find, and not one of her textbooks was available in raised print. Annie had to read them to her. Annie had to look up words that were new to Helen, whether in French, German, or Latin — languages Annie knew nothing about. She had to attend every class Helen went to, spelling into her hand whatever the teacher said. Mr. Gilman learned the manual language, as did Frau Groete, the German instructor, but otherwise the burden was always and entirely on Annie.

It was a heavy burden. Although Annie never complained about the strain on her eyes, Helen was beginning to understand at what cost this education of hers was being bought.

Yet they never seriously considered giving it up — as far as Annie was concerned, her own reputation was at stake, as well as Helen's. Besides, Helen loved it, loved the hard work, the languages, the ancient history, everything except mathematics. In Latin she was said to be quicker and more precise than the average student. In German, "Helen has always a clear, beautiful accurate picture of the thing that she is reading or describing," Frau Groete reported. "Very often other girls give a great many words and say nothing; Helen never."

Yet for Annie and Gilman alike, there was one important question that had no answer: how many years would it take to prepare Helen for Radcliffe? Five? Four, or even as few as three?

Christmas came, bringing Mrs. Keller, Mildred, and the baby of the family, Phillips Brooks. Helen was so happy to have them with her that Mr. Gilman agreed to let Mildred stay on as a pupil. And when it was time for final exams, he arranged for Helen to have a separate room where she could use her typewriter without disturbing the others. Annie was banished from that room, and a guard stood outside the door as extra insurance that nobody and nothing interfered. Gilman administered the exams himself in the manual language.

Helen came through triumphantly; successful in every subject, she took honors in English and German. "The result is remarkable," Gilman reported. "I think I may say that no candidate in Harvard or Radcliffe was graded higher than Helen in English." Together with Annie, she spent the summer at the family home of Joseph Edgar Chamberlin, an editor of *Youth's Companion* and a friend since Helen's first article for the magazine, in Wrentham, a little country town on a lake. There was boating and swimming, and when Uncle Ed Chamberlin took her for walks through the forest he talked about things that mattered to him — politics, justice, socialism.

Helen was seventeen years old now, with thick brown hair and a clear, healthy complexion. It was obvious from her eyes that they were blind, but otherwise she was a lively and attractive young person. She dressed the way her classmates dressed, and she enjoyed using their schoolgirl slang. A reporter who interviewed her at Wrentham noted, "Her enthusiasm for Radcliffe is most inspiring. If a Radcliffe student calls upon her her expressive face lights up, and she says eagerly, 'So you study at Radcliffe.'"

When the new term started Helen learned she would be taking Greek, Latin, French, physics, geometry, algebra, and astronomy — twenty-seven recitations a week, each lasting half an hour. In a very short time, debates over the weight of this program developed into a pitched battle between Annie and Gilman.

Helen's classes were so much larger than the first year's that none of the teachers could give her special instruction. There was a new machine for Brailling algebra, and she had to learn to use it, also how to construct geometrical figures with a cushion and wires. Helen never had much sympathy with mathematics in any of its forms, and geometry in particular was a trial for her. There were times when all her courage drained away, when she was frightened and angry and ashamed of her anger after it passed.

Yet Annie was convinced that all would come right

in the end, that Helen would master these difficulties, as she had mastered others. Gilman begged to differ. He and Annie had originally agreed that this second year's curriculum should be a light one for Helen, but when she succeeded so well with her exams, Annie came up with another plan. She wanted Helen to finish her college preparation the following year — meaning, after a total of three years. It was the barest minimum that Annie and Gilman had ever considered.

He was most reluctant, but said it could be tried. The result was the overloaded schedule with which Helen started her second year.

Mrs. Hopkins came for a visit in November, saw Helen, and was thoroughly alarmed. In a letter to Gilman, she said the child was "in what I might term a state of collapse. . . . I think Helen is studying too hard." She spent her Saturdays and Sundays at work, which meant she was deprived of the companionship of her classmates, the girls she had started school with; she missed them and longed for them. "For me to feel that Helen is not happy is like crushing my heart," Mrs. Hopkins went on. Why did Mr. Gilman allow such a state of affairs?

Gilman wrote back, explaining that the change of

program was Miss Sullivan's idea, not his. As for her loneliness, that too was Miss Sullivan's doing — partly because Helen was made to work so hard, partly because, at Miss Sullivan's insistence, they were now living in a different residence hall from the others.

Mrs. Hopkins urged Gilman to ignore Miss Sullivan if he could not change her, and do whatever he thought best.

Dr. Bell came unexpectedly. Gilman told him Helen was in bed, had spent the whole weekend in bed, apparently worn out. The two men stepped in for a chat with her. Dr. Bell told Annie that Helen did not look well, that she was overworking; her health, and perhaps her life, were at stake, he said.

None of this registered on Annie, who stubbornly insisted that Helen was fine and healthy and would rise to every challenge, the harder the better. Arthur Gilman, seriously shaken by now, appealed directly to Mrs. Keller. In a letter that must have stunned her, he said the teachers had been warning him about Helen, that her work had fallen off, that her health was uncertain, and that Miss Sullivan seemed unaware of the danger.

Mrs. Keller wrote immediately to Gilman and

Annie, saying Helen's program must be cut back to what she could do without danger to her health. Sleepless, troubled by guilt, Kate wondered if she herself was at fault, if she had unwisely given too much authority to Miss Annie — whom she loved and admired, who had done such wonders for Helen's mind, but who had apparently ignored her physical well-being.

Now that he had Mrs. Keller's solid support, Gilman felt free to act. Geometry and astronomy must be taken out of Helen's program. First, he told Miss Sullivan about it. Then, a week later, he set it down formally on paper, "in order that there may be no doubt in the matter. . . . I have seen too many bright girls injured by overstudy to permit Helen to risk the penalty that would follow." It must have seemed to him that the weight of a terrible responsibility was now lifted from his shoulders.

He had made an enemy of Annie Sullivan in the process, however. Although she said she accepted the change, she threatened several times to leave, sometimes with Helen, sometimes without her. Teachers reported that she was impatient with Helen. Annie herself told Gilman she was irritated by the "stupidity" that Helen showed at times.

Helen said nothing about her teacher's impatience or irritability, at least not in her accounts of the Cambridge School. Yet she was not unaware of Annie's difficult nature, the temper, the "impetuosity . . . likely to burst forth at the first sign of dullness in [myself] or anyone else." Once she described Annie as holding "her darker moods well in hand like an animal trainer."

But Annie's faults never mattered to Helen — who recognized them, and did her best to put them out of her mind. They were far outweighed by Annie's virtues, the most important being that she had opened the world to Helen, and that she continued to sacrifice her eyesight for Helen. Besides, Helen loved her, and love excuses everything.

As for the change of program — the lightened workload, with graduation a year later than the rest of her class — Helen perceived it as a hurtful mistake: "I could scarcely endure my bitter humiliation; it seemed to me as if I had been cheated out of my proper share in the schoolwork. I knew that [Miss Sullivan] . . . had loved me and taken the best care of me for nearly eleven years, and that no harm had come to me while I was with her. She has worked all those long years to make my life sweet and happy."

Now the teachers' complaints grew more urgent. They said they could no longer endure Miss Sullivan. Remarks she made in the hearing of teachers and pupils in the classroom and of Mildred and the servants in the residence hall, were "exceedingly unfortunate." The woman in charge of Howells House went so far as to say she would prefer that Miss Sullivan should never be in the presence of her girls because she said things critical of Mr. Gilman and didn't care who heard her. Annie often boasted that she had complete power over Helen, that she could take her from the school at any moment, transfer her to Europe or elsewhere, and in fact do whatever she pleased without consulting Mrs. Keller.

It was the opinion of these teachers, and of Gilman, too, that Annie was better adapted to the training of a schoolgirl than that of a young lady who had already far outstripped her intellectually. So Gilman informed Mrs. Keller. And by the start of December, he was pleading with her to come to Cambridge, to see for herself the situation Annie Sullivan had created. If worse came to worst, he said, it might be necessary for her to remove both daughters from the school. But she must come.

It seemed that Kate could no longer avoid what she most feared, a confrontation with Miss Annie. She sent three letters to Gilman, then fired off a telegram authorizing him to act as Helen's guardian. For some reason, none of these communications reached Cambridge, so she wrote again: "Miss Sullivan had a hard and bitter childhood and that has been one other reason that I have tried always to make her stay with Helen pleasant."

On the eighth of December, Kate's telegram — the one giving Mr. Gilman authority to act as Helen's guardian — was finally delivered. He showed it to Annie. She took it to mean that she must go away and never come back, leaving Helen in the care of her newly appointed guardian, Arthur Gilman.

Until that day, Helen knew only that Gilman and Annie disagreed about how hard she ought to work, but she had no way of knowing the intensity of their feelings. If Annie's fingers jabbed impatiently when they spoke into Helen's hand, if her footsteps were harsh and hurried, there might be many reasons for it. Or no reason. Annie had moods, that was all.

But on the day her mother's telegram arrived, Helen sat next to Annie in class, touched her hand, felt it tremble, and recognized disaster. "What is it, Teacher?" she asked with alarm. "Helen, I fear we are going to be separated!" "What! Separated? What do you mean?"

As Helen remembered it, Annie "said something about a letter . . . from someone who expressed his opinion to my mother that Miss Sullivan and I should be separated. Mr. Gilman, whom I had trusted, had done it all."

That same morning Annie left Helen, Mildred, and the school, and escaped "to our true friends, Mr. and Mrs. Richard Derby Fuller of Boston." This part of the story is told in *Teacher*, Helen's biography of Annie. "She was overcome with despair. As she approached the Charles River an almost overmastering impulse seized her to throw herself into the water, but it seemed to her that an angel laid a restraining hand upon her and said, 'Not yet.' . . . It was a time of heartbreak."

The Fullers were horrified to learn that Helen might be separated from Annie. They advised her to send telegrams to her mother, to Dr. Bell, and to Uncle Ed Chamberlin at Wrentham. The Fullers themselves wrote to Mrs. Hutton, who managed the fund that paid for Helen's schooling, and Mrs. Hutton wrote immediately to Gilman: "Against this action . . . Mr. Hutton and I must protest in the very strongest terms. Mrs. Keller must realize how peculiarly strong is the tie which binds pupil and teacher. . . ."

Gilman's response was confusion. Having done what he honestly believed to be right, he had spent all his emotional energy in the process, and had nothing left for the aftermath. Helen, sobbing most of the time and close to hysteria, clung to Mildred, who was also sobbing. They were unable to sleep that first night; when morning came, they were unable to eat, and there was no question of Helen's going to classes.

Annie returned in the course of the day, demanding that Gilman allow her to see Helen. He refused at first, but Annie could not be made to leave, and eventually he gave in. Uncle Ed Chamberlin arrived later, and with Gilman's permission brought Helen, Mildred, and Annie home with him.

"At Wrentham I took Helen alone in my study, and told her it might soon be incumbent on her to decide whether she would stay with Annie or go away from her with her mother." This was Chamberlin's recollection of that afternoon, some thirty years later. "She said to me, 'Uncle Ed, if I have to decide between my mother and Teacher, I will stay with Teacher.' This decided me as to my own sympathies in the case."

Helen was badly frightened. The telegrams she sent to friends reverberated with her fears — in one of them, "they are trying to take my dear teacher from me! My heart is broken. You know what she has been to me — You know how dearly and truly we have always loved each other. Oh, dear friend, help us!"

Mrs. Keller arrived at last, embraced her daughters, wept with them, and conferred with the friends who had gathered at the Chamberlins' home. What happened during the next several days is only partly known, but there is no question about the ending. In a total reversal of her previous position, Kate sent Gilman a brief note, cool and distant in tone, telling him her daughters were now formally withdrawing from his school.

The drama had played itself out. Its theme was that Helen and Annie could not and would not be separated. Some of those who were close to Helen believed separation might be a good idea, but they weren't in Wrentham discussing Helen's fate. None of the people gathered there could bear to see her wounded, even though such a wound might ultimately lead to a more independent life — just as no one was willing to see Annie cast off and set adrift. She was in her early thirties; she too could have made another life. But it didn't happen that way. Nobody had the stomach for it.

nine

THE ASSAULT ON RADCLIFFE

$\mathcal{A}$ private tutor was found, a Mr. Merton Keith of Cambridge. He agreed to come once a week to Wrentham, where Helen and Annie were staying with the Chamberlins.

They were a large, active, extroverted family. All the young people spoke so distinctly that Helen had no trouble reading their lips with her fingers, and one of the daughters learned the manual language. They had snowball fights, and they walked across the frozen pond, sometimes tobogganing on it. One person would balance the sled on the crest of a hill, as Helen recalled. The others would climb aboard, "and when we are ready, off we dash down the side of the hill in a headlong rush, and, leaping a projection, plunge into a snowdrift and go skimming far across the pond at a tremendous rate!"

But the real business of her life at this point was study — cramming — for the exams she must pass to enter Radcliffe. When the new tutor came they worked together for three and a half hours at a stretch, then Helen was left with a week's worth of lessons to finish before the next session. Keith was a youngish man, dark-eyed, with a bushy mustache he may have grown in the hope of looking older. He was capable, conscientious, and unsentimental.

Keith had been assigned to teach four subjects: Greek, Latin, algebra, and geometry. They started with Greek, and by the end of four months Helen had translated and written out about one thousand sentences from Greek into English and six hundred sentences from English into Greek. Keith believed that within a very short time she would be reading Homer with pleasure.

Mathematics was another story. Friends wanted to know if there was any point to her going on with it, any hope of success in the entrance exams. The dean of Radcliffe was appealed to. The dean suggested that Helen might be allowed to substitute other subjects "more congenial to her."

Helen refused to do any substituting. She never enjoyed mathematics, couldn't see the use of it, and said so. But she considered it a challenge, and would have been mortified at having to give it up. "Her ambition and her confidence in her own power to master whatever she has once undertaken are two of her most marked traits of mind," according to Keith. So they attacked geometry, using the system of bent wires and cushions that revealed to Helen the geometrical shapes others were able to see. Then, as Keith recalled, "She had to carry in her mind the lettering of the figures, the hypothesis and conclusion, the construction, and the process of proof. To keep the mind clear under such conditions is very hard. After seeing through the proof, perhaps by many trials, she had to record the results by her typewriter for the examiner. This in itself is a great task to do accurately."

What was Annie up to, while Helen did battle with geometry? Anxious and depressed at first, devastated by the ordeal at the Cambridge School — when for at least a moment she had been suicidal — Annie spent months reclaiming her peace of mind. But it did return, and by spring she was laughing and flirting with the young men who came and went from the Chamberlins' home. "The future was uncertain," Helen wrote, in describing her teacher during that time, "but her doubts concerning me were lessening, and her grasp upon life was growing firmer. . . . *and she ceased to treat me as a child, she did not command me anymore.*"

In the journal Helen kept that winter, there are

other signs that childhood was behind her. The physical changes had been apparent for some years. Now the inner changes that come with adolescence finally — belatedly — arrived on the scene: restlessness, seesawing between joy and the depths of misery, the sense of being a stranger to her own self.

As a child she had faced life with radiant optimism. Now Helen wrote in her journal, "This morning I had no taste for breakfast, and I've had to use all my conscience (what's conscience anyway?) to keep myself at the helm of duty. Why doesn't it help me that I've done my work nicely? I simply despise the spirit in which I've gone about my work. . . . When shall I ever get out of me? I'm tired of all my failures, fruitless resolutions. I'm tired of always fearing that I shall be stupid or do something clumsy or careless. . . . My character seems no good, and it will cost me a long, long effort to build it up."

Later, in the same journal: "I haven't done well in Algebra, and my temper has been unmanageable. I am usually willing to persevere, but I wouldn't today because I was treated so much like — well — a naughty child. . . . Something in me resists fiercely, and I can't explain it."

The winter ended, and spring brought the college entrance exams, which would take place in June at Radcliffe. Mr. Keith and Helen had always assumed that someone would read the questions to her the way Gilman used to, in the manual language. Since Keith had never learned it, he thought Miss Sullivan was the logical choice. But no, the college authorities refused to have Miss Sullivan anywhere near the room during exams — instead, they would be translated into Braille. Eugene Vining, a teacher at Perkins, would do the translating.

A few days before the exam, Mr. Vining sent Helen a Brailled copy of an old Harvard paper in algebra. There were several kinds of Braille in use at the time — American, English, and New York Point — and Helen was familiar with all of them. But in math, she had always used English Braille, while Vining used American. The systems were quite different.

She wrote to him, explaining the problem, and by return mail he sent a table of signs that she learned, or thought she learned. But on the night before the start of exams, she found herself unable to distinguish bracket, brace, radical, and the various combinations of the three. Suppose she failed, bringing disgrace on herself and Teacher? She knew there were a number of people eager to see Annie Sullivan humiliated, and she promised herself she wouldn't allow it to happen.

Elementary Greek and advanced Latin were given on the first day, and Helen felt thoroughly at ease with them. But the second day brought geometry, then algebra. She had forgotten her watch, one specially designed for the blind, and without it she had no way of pacing herself. Even worse, the signs that she thought she knew somehow made no sense. Confused, fighting off panic, she managed to work through to the end.

Ten days later, Helen learned she had passed every subject, and passed "with credit in advanced Latin." When Mr. Keith heard the news, he called it an impressive achievement, "a triumph of ambition stimulated by obstacles." But Helen's reaction was not triumphant. "I was bitterly disappointed not to have done better," she told him, "and my disappointment often throws a shadow upon the pleasure which the summer is bringing me. . . ."

On July 4, 1899, a formal certificate of admission to the freshman class of Radcliffe was sent to Helen Adams Keller, but she did not enter that fall. Agnes Irwin, the dean of the college, was against it. Miss Irwin advised Helen to take a special course instead, one that concentrated on her own individual strengths — writing, for example. And Helen was persuaded, or half-persuaded.

Annie was not. Annie was up in arms. Helen was not wanted at Radcliffe, she said, because she had not done well enough on the entrance exams — and the reason for that was a "conspiracy." Mr. Gilman had conspired with others to lower Helen's marks, so that she had honors only in Latin, when she should have had honors in several subjects. In Annie's opinion Mr. Gilman was responsible for everything.

But there was no need for a conspiracy to keep Helen out of Radcliffe. Cambridge was a small town, everybody in it must have known about Annie and the Cambridge School. To accept Helen as a student would mean accepting the presence of Annie Sullivan — the same Miss Sullivan who had reduced Arthur Gilman, a founder of Radcliffe, to a quivering jelly. Meanwhile, Cornell University and the University of Chicago would be happy to have Miss Keller as a student, accompanied, of course, by Miss Sullivan.

Single-minded and persistent, Helen said it was Radcliffe or nothing. When President Woodrow

Wilson asked her, many years later, why she had insisted on that one college, she answered: "Because they didn't want me at Radcliffe, and, being stubborn, I chose to override their objections."

Helen and Annie found a place to stay in Cambridge, and Mr. Keith came every afternoon. In a letter to Mildred, Helen said she was "studying English history, English literature, French and Latin, and by and by I shall take up German and English composition — let us groan!" This was followed by news about "a swell winter outfit," coats, hats, and two dresses made by a French dressmaker; one was green wool, the top trimmed with pink and green brocaded velvet. Teacher had two new dresses as well.

In May 1900, Helen prepared to storm the walls of Radcliffe a second time. Writing to its academic board, she said she was ready for regular courses now, and although she said it most politely the message was clear: I have passed the exams, and am entitled to admission. Admit me.

A month went by without an answer. And then there was an answer: Helen Adams Keller had been formally accepted into the class of 1904. When word of this acceptance became public, according to one of the Perkins teachers, "there was much talk — 'Why don't they say outright that Miss Sullivan is entering Radcliffe instead of Helen Keller, a blind, deaf and dumb girl!'"

Perhaps it was in response to such talk that Dean Irwin proclaimed certain rules: Miss Sullivan was to leave the building at the very moment the messenger carrying exams from Harvard to Radcliffe started out. Furthermore, whenever exams took place, the dean was going to pay, out of her own pocket, for two proctors; one would proctor Helen, the other would proctor Helen's proctor. An experienced Braille typist would be present at every exam, to transcribe the questions as soon as they reached the room containing Helen and her proctors. If Helen had any questions, the Braille typist would answer them in the manual language — and every word must also be spoken aloud so the proctor could record it.

Once these safeguards had been declared and accepted, Radcliffe was ready for Helen Keller. Certainly Helen was ready. Since childhood she had dreamed of college as a series of long, golden days filled with learning, thinking, reading. The teachers would be philosopher-kings. The girls her own age would be her companions, sharing lessons, confiding in her, drawing her into their beautifully normal lives.

"In the wonderland of Mind," she said, "I should be as free as another."

{ ten }

INSIDE THE IVORY TOWER

"*T*oday I took luncheon with the Freshman Class of Radcliffe," Helen wrote in a theme for English composition. "I had the opportunity to make friends with all my classmates, and the pleasure of knowing that they regarded me as one of themselves, instead of thinking of me as living apart and taking no interest in the everyday nothings of life, as I had sometimes feared they did. I have often been surprised to hear this opinion expressed or rather implied by girls of my own age. . . . Once someone wrote to me that in his mind I was always 'sweet and earnest, thinking only of what is wise, good and interesting.' . . . I always laugh at these foolish notions. . . . but even while I laugh I feel a twinge of pain in my heart."

The pain refused to go away. Helen's freshman year was haunted by an underlying note of sorrow that was partly loneliness, partly disillusionment with college. She was reminded of library bookshelves at the Cambridge School: "When my teacher and I first saw them she exclaimed, 'What beautiful books! Just feel them.' I touched the handsome volumes and read some of the titles, which were so richly embossed that I could distinguish the letters. But when I tried to take one of them down I found that they were imitation books, all bound and lettered in gold to look like Chaucer, Montaigne, Bacon, Shakespeare, and Dante. That is the way I felt as the days in college passed, and my dreams faded."

As for the loneliness, it came and went and came again. Helen tried, as she had always tried, to convince herself that in spite of its limitations her life was rich and full. This was not self-deception, but a way of surviving — she would "fight it out to the end with a smiling face," she once said, and she would do it without complaint, without surrendering to fate.

Now she rode through the streets of Cambridge with Annie on her tandem bicycle. She played chess and checkers with her classmates and went swimming with them. From time to time, one or another of the students would bring her flowers or a box of candy, and Helen would throw her arms around the girl, kissing her the way she used to kiss and embrace everyone she met as a child. But hardly anyone knew the manual alphabet. "Hearing" them by touching their faces meant she had to speak to them with her voice, and she knew it was a crippled voice. So heart-to-heart confidences — even ordinary conversations — were difficult, yet they were what she longed for.

She moved through rooms and corridors that were crowded with girls. She sensed their presence, felt the vibrations of their footsteps, smelled the ironed-in starch of their shirtwaist blouses, the soap or toilet water that scented their skin. At most she got a quick handshake as they moved on. Some may have been awed by her celebrity. Or by the strangeness — the eeriness — of coming face-to-face with a person who could neither see nor hear them, and who seemed to belong to an alien species.

The result, Helen found, was that "a sense of isolation enfolds me like a cold mist as I sit alone and wait at life's shut door. Beyond there is light, and music, and sweet companionship; but I may not enter. Fate, silent, pitiless, bars the way."

Annie and Helen had been allowed to room off campus, and they found a rental house where they were cared for by an Irish maid, Bridget Crimmins. They enjoyed a degree of freedom that was impossible for other students, yet the charming little house, with its view of trees and fields and the Charles River in the distance, only increased Helen's separation from her sister students in the dormitory.

Even during classes, when seated in the midst of her classmates, she felt almost alone. "The professor is as remote as if he were talking through a telephone," she said. "The lectures are spelled into my hand as rapidly as possible, and . . . words rush through my hand like hounds in pursuit of a hare which they often miss."

Helen had insisted on carrying a full academic load: French, German, history, English composition, and English literature. Since she was unable to take notes, she typed out everything she could remember after she got home, using her Braille machine. For other work — exercises, daily themes, tests, mid-year exams, whatever the professor would have to read — she used a Hammond typewriter, with movable-type shuttles for Greek, French, or Latin.

As before, Annie read to her and looked up words in French or German dictionaries. But there were many more books now, all unwieldy and heavy, and every-thing took so long. In one of the daily themes Helen handed in for English 22, she said there were disad-vantages to going to college. "The one I feel most is

lack of time. I used to have time to think, to reflect —
my mind and I." College left no time for thinking or
dreaming. College was a race, an obstacle course, the
end result of it was a brain stuffed with miscellaneous
information.

Helen's opinion of college never improved; if anything, it became increasingly negative. And yet there
were certain instructors who were more than voices
speaking through a microphone. "Copey" — Dr.
Charles Copeland — was one. Copey endeared himself to Helen by treating her the way he treated
everyone, criticizing her severely, sarcastically, as few
teachers dared to do.

He expected his students to hand in daily themes,
to be read, evaluated, and then returned. In Copey's
opinion, Helen Keller was the best writer of freshman
English themes he had come across, either at Radcliffe
or Harvard. But at the same time, he was aware of
something lacking, something personal, immediate.
He wanted to hear more about her, less about what she
had learned from books, and he told her so.

Helen was so stung by this reproof that for a time
she stopped writing themes. Then she sent a letter to
Dr. Copeland: "I have never been satisfied with my

work," she said, "but I never knew what my difficulty was until you pointed it out to me. When I came to your class last October, I was trying with all my might to be like everybody else, to forget as entirely as possible my limitations. . . . Now, however, I see the folly of attempting to hitch one's wagon to a star with harness that does not belong to it." From then on she was resolved to be herself, she said, to live her own life and write her own thoughts.

It wasn't easy. Helen continued to agonize over her theme-writing. She was slow, she claimed, she had a slow, halting mind. She was a total mediocrity, uninteresting and unpromising. When she tried to write, ideas obstinately refused to flow. In fact she found writing a burden, not a pleasure, "and at times I HATE it. . . . It is this difficulty and NO OTHER that foils my efforts and frustrates the most ardent wishes of [Miss Sullivan] and myself . . . and makes me vicious at times." Yet she did write themes, and submitted most of them. And it was her work that Copey read aloud to the class with more than usual pleasure.

Freshman year led inevitably to finals — a serial nightmare, with Helen continually amazed at all the things she knew that were not on the exam. Yet she passed in everything. That first year had been filled with disillusionment and loneliness, but it was over, done with; the future could only be an improvement on it. She had the summer to recover.

The Chamberlins were at Wrentham, not far away, and always welcoming. Nina Rhoades, a close friend Helen's age, who was blind and lived in New York, persuaded her to visit often. And in Cambridge, a social circle of sorts had grown up around Annie and the rented house; it consisted of young men from Harvard and MIT. Looking back on those years, Helen wrote about long evenings when she sat before an open fire "with a circle of eager, imaginative students, drinking cider, popping corn, and joyously tearing to pieces society, philosophies, religions, and literatures. We stripped everything to the naked skeletons."

The first beginnings of her political beliefs can be glimpsed in these discussions. There is something else as well, something that seems to glide in and out of her memories — never fully explained, only hinted at.

A young man named Carl, who fed squirrels with her as they sat by the roadside and counted birds, tried to tap into her hand the sounds the birds made when singing. A young man named Patrick also appears, then he and Carl melt into the crowd of others and are never mentioned again. But the subject of men — men her own age, and Helen's interest in them — would be discussed at greater length during the course of that summer.

With Annie, she was invited for a long visit to Alexander Graham Bell and his family at their country home in Nova Scotia. One evening Dr. Bell and Helen stood together on the piazza; taking her hand in his, he told her, "It seems to me, Helen, a day must come when love, which is more than friendship, will knock at the door of your heart and demand to be let in."

"What made you think of that?"

"Oh, I often think of your future. To me you are a sweet, desirable young girl, and it is natural to think about love and happiness when we are young."

"I do think of love sometimes," she confessed, "but it is like a beautiful flower which I may not touch, but whose fragrance makes the garden a place of delight just the same." She couldn't imagine a man wanting to marry her, she went on; it would seem like marrying a statue.

He patted her hand. "You are very young. If a good man should desire to make you his wife, don't let anyone persuade you to forego that happiness because of your peculiar handicap."

Helen was greatly relieved when Mrs. Bell and Annie joined them and the discussion of love and marriage came to an end.

{eleven}

THE STORY OF MY LIFE

One morning, a few weeks after the start of Helen's sophomore year, she was called out of Latin class to meet someone by the name of William Alexander — an editor of *Ladies' Home Journal*, as it turned out. He said the magazine wanted to publish the story of her life in monthly installments. She would be handsomely paid.

But that was out of the question, Helen explained; her college work was all she could manage.

"You have already written a considerable part of it in your themes," he said, which took her by surprise.

"How in the world did you find out I was writing themes?"

He laughed and told her it was an editor's business to be well informed. And it would be the easiest thing in the world, he went on, to transform those themes into magazine articles.

Without a clear idea of what she was getting into, Helen soon found herself signing a contract that promised *Ladies' Home Journal* her life's story, in monthly installments, for the sum of three thousand dollars.

Three thousand dollars! In her imagination the story was already written, already a classic. Money, success, fame — she was dazzled.

Perhaps it was Dr. Copeland who told the editor about Helen's themes, and suggested this autobiography in installments. But Annie too must have been partly responsible, for Helen would never have accepted unless Annie agreed.

Little else of interest was going on in Annie's life at the time, only the grinding labor of getting Helen through her classes and through the mountain of homework. As for the classes themselves, Annie had had her fill of them. "Three times a week I drink in desperation at every pore," she said, in describing Helen's Shakespeare class.

But an autobiography, one whose writing she could counsel and encourage, promised excitement. With the generous payment dancing like gold at the rainbow's end, the two of them set to work, Helen as writer, Annie as counselor and critic.

By December, the first installment was finished — Helen's infancy, her illness and isolation, the coming of Annie, the "miracle" at the well-house. Most of this material came straight from the daily themes that Dr.

Copeland had read and criticized, and Helen used his suggestions for improving them. The editors of the *Journal* were delighted with the result. It would appear in their April issue, and in the meantime they looked forward eagerly to the second installment.

On her Braille machine, Helen had written about one hundred pages of notes and episodes, and they became the basis for Chapter Two. Although it skipped back and forth in time, and lacked any description of her early training in language, she knew these matters could be cleared up later.

The *Journal* expressed dismay. They needed a coherent second installment they said, with a clear narrative line, and they needed it now.

Helen realized she was in trouble — "in deep water, and frightened out of my wits," as she put it. "I was utterly inexperienced in the preparation of magazine articles. I did not know how to cut my material to fit the given space. I had no idea that the time limit was of such importance until telegrams began to come, thick and fast. . . . Special delivery letters filled the chorus of dismay: 'We must have the next chapter immediately.' 'There is no connection between page six and page seven. Wire the missing part.'"

Annie tried to help, but knew nothing about editing. And Curtis Bok, the *Journal's* publisher, saw he had made a serious mistake in printing the first of a series before he got his hands on the rest. It was then that one of Helen's friends brought up the name of John Macy. Twenty-five years old, he came from a distinguished, but no longer prosperous, New England family, and had gone through Harvard on a scholarship. He taught English literature there and held a second job as well, working for *Youth's Companion* as an associate editor.

When Annie and Helen met him they found him likable — tall, pleasant-looking, with a certain sweetness of manner, and a mind both vigorous and original. Helen took to him immediately, Annie somewhat more slowly. When they agreed to work with him, he learned the manual language.

Together with Annie, Mr. Macy read the disconnected passages of the manuscript, put them in chronological order, and counted the words. It was done with Miss Keller beside them, as he explained, "referring everything, especially matters of phrasing, to her for revision. We read to her the sentences on each side of a gap and took down the connecting sentences that she supplied."

The sense of crisis receded. Succeeding monthly installments began arriving in the *Journal*'s offices. By August, the final installment was on the newsstands.

From first to last, the public took Helen's story to its heart — and, as it happened, she was about to meet an even wider audience, for now John Macy transformed himself into a literary agent, intent on selling the magazine articles for publication as a book.

There would be three parts. First, Helen's autobiography as it appeared in the *Journal*. Second, a selection of her letters from childhood on. The third part was a narrative that had never been seen before, one as compelling as any work of fiction — Annie's letters to Mrs. Hopkins, describing her teaching methods as they evolved. After correcting Annie's spelling and grammar, Mr. Macy wove the letters into a consecutive whole, so that the reader could follow, day by day and in Annie's own words, a heroic act of rescue, carried out by a very young woman with only herself to rely on.

Then John Macy set to work finding a publisher. Although he had no experience along those lines, he carried out the task with the same assurance he brought to editing. In April 1902 the three of them — Helen, Annie, and John Macy — signed a contract with the firm of Doubleday, Page, for a book Helen would call *The Story of My Life*.

When it was published in March 1903 — Helen's junior year in college, the year of her twenty-third birthday — critics and readers alike were enchanted. *The Century* found it "unique in the world's literature." The *San Francisco Chronicle* praised Helen's style as being "full of force, individuality, and charm." The *Literary Digest* noted the absence of "morbidness or self-pity."

The chorus of praise was not universal. Mr. Macy's friends were convinced he had not only edited the book, but written it. People who disliked Annie Sullivan disliked her even more because it was her point of view — not theirs — that Helen presented. And an eminent German teacher of the deaf-blind, Rudolph Brohman, insisted "*The Story of My Life* by Helen Keller is mainly the work of her teacher, Miss Sullivan."

When the book failed to sell as well that first year as John Macy had hoped, the publisher assured him it would live "on and on and on, and there is no book I feel prouder of." Of course he was right, for *The Story of My Life* has been translated into well over fifty languages, including Chinese, Japanese, Korean, Gujarati,

Tamil, Pashto and Cebuano. People of all ages have been finding inspiration in it for nearly a century.

For Helen and Annie, the book brought freedom. They had money; they could spend it on good clothes, which both adored, on travel, and on improvements to an old farmhouse in Wrentham that Annie bought with some of the stock John Spaulding had given them. Helen felt independent now, confirmed in her belief that women could and should pay their own way.

All this time, while the book was being written, published, and reviewed, she had kept up her college studies. It was her intention to excel at Radcliffe. This was Annie's intention as well; in fact, Annie counted on Helen to rise to the topmost level of academic performance, and repeatedly told her so.

Helen was still uncertain that her college studies — literature, Latin, philosophy — mattered very much. The real world mattered. She needed to be part of it, to carry her full share of it, as much as her disabilities permitted. To Helen, this meant having work to do, for a human being who does not work "is not a member of society, and can have no standing in it," she said.

"To be so imbecile as not to know how to work . . . so crippled or defective as not to be able to work, makes life a burden." And Radcliffe was not preparing her for real work in the real world.

For Annie, who had until now been a victim of overwork, there was a welcome change. She had help now from John Macy, who was no longer Mr. Macy to them, but John. He did much of the reading for Helen that Annie had once done. He consulted dictionaries for her, studied with her, helped her with her philosophy course and with whatever else she needed help. With Helen and Annie went to their Wrentham farm for Easter vacation, John was there almost every night.

Passages he wrote for the third section of Helen's autobiography reveal some of his feelings at the time. He spoke of Miss Sullivan's "intelligence, wisdom, sagacity, unremitting perseverance and unbending will." She was "a person of extraordinary power," he said. Her mind, which was vigorous and original, "has lent much of its vitality to her pupil."

He admired Miss Keller, but Annie Sullivan bowled him over. He was in love, had fallen into love within months of their first meeting, and Annie loved him in return. She was ten years older and had other claims on her heart in the form of a beloved foster child. But there it was. Whatever course Helen's life might take after graduation, she would have to deal with the challenges brought about by this unexpected romance.

And in the meantime, there was the matter of graduation. The ceremony should have been a triumphal march from classroom to platform, where the longed-for diploma would be put in Helen's hand. Unfortunately, it was not a triumphal march, but rather a series of hesitant steps, forward, backward, forward again, an embarrassed shuffle carried out in the full glare of publicity.

In early June, a Boston newspaper announced, "Helen Keller to receive magna cum laude degree." Honors that accompany the college degree can take one of three forms: summa cum laude, with highest praise; magna cum laude, with great praise; and cum laude, with praise. It was an era when a young woman was lucky to get all the way through high school. In 1900, for example, for every ten boys or girls of high-school age, only one was actually in school. Graduating from an elite college like Radcliffe was therefore a great distinction — and in Helen's case, graduating from any college at all would be nothing less than history-making. So the news that Helen Keller was to earn her Radcliffe degree magna cum laude must have been barely credible to some people, perhaps a mistake or an exaggeration. It was repeated in newspapers throughout the country.

Two weeks into June, in the Boston *Transcript*, Miss Keller sent word that "illness prevented her leaving her home in Wrentham." In another paper, "Disappointed in not obtaining the highest honors and fatigued from her four years of hard work, Miss Keller has retired from all the social festivities connected with her graduation . . . [and] from the marks already in it looks as if Miss Keller will fail to receive a magna." From Chicago: "Helen Keller breaks down — gifted student on verge of prostration."

One thing was clear: She would take no part in the Class Day celebrations. Perhaps she might not even attend her own graduation, although this was less clear. "Her insatiable ambition prompted her to try for the highest goal," according to the Boston *American*, "and, failing by a short margin she remains inconsolable." Which seems like an accurate summing up of this sorry affair — and yet, Helen did come, after all.

On the day of her twenty-fourth birthday, she arrived with Annie in time to take her place in the line of ninety-six graduating seniors, all in caps and gowns. Mrs. Keller had been unable to attend because of illness at home. But a family friend was there, watching as the seniors climbed the steps to the stage. They bowed to the college official when their names were called out, then came forward to receive their diplomas from President LeBaron Briggs. Ripples of applause and excited hand-waves greeted each of the graduates.

Then Helen climbed to the stage, guided as always by Annie. The family friend recalled that when she stepped forward to receive her diploma — cum laude, with praise — the scattered applause became an ovation. But as soon as the ceremonies were over, Helen and Annie vanished. People who wanted to extend their congratulations searched for them in vain.

Helen wrote many years later about her teacher's "disappointment over my failure to attain the highest honors in every subject I studied. She was ... overwrought by my apparent lack of zeal in obtaining the summa." Helen never says whether she herself was disappointed — but she does tell us she had felt deeply injured on her teacher's behalf. Radcliffe had failed to recognize how much Annie contributed to Helen's education; they failed even to recognize Annie's existence. "The pain caused by that indifference or thoughtlessness is still a thorn in my memory," Helen said, more than twenty-five years later.

Radcliffe might have answered that they never wanted Miss Sullivan to begin with, and never pretended otherwise. They might also have pointed out that Miss Sullivan was openly scornful of academic learning, and therefore learned nothing herself. Yet the disappointments Helen and Annie felt were real and poignant, and the day that should have been joyful for both of them was thoroughly spoiled. They fled from it to the comfort of Wrentham.

In looking back at her Radcliffe years, Helen often said that Dean Irwin had been right after all, that there was no need for her to go to college. But she had happier thoughts on the subject as well. Just before graduation, in a speech to the alumnae association, she said, "College has breathed new life into my mind. . . . I grow stronger in the conviction that there is nothing good or right which we cannot accomplish if we have the will to strive. . . . The end of my school days fills me with bright anticipations. The doors of the bright world are flung open before me and a light shines upon me, the light kindled by the thought that there is something for me to do beyond the threshold."

{ twelve }

WE THREE

Wrentham was a country village an hour's ride by streetcar from Boston, and their house stood on seven acres of neglected land at the end of a pretty street. It was big, rambling, and very old. John Macy spent his vacation cleaning the barn out, fixing the barn doors, and making a bookcase that he sawed, planed, and painted.

Local workmen transformed two pantries and a dairy room into a study for Helen, then built a long balcony outside her second-floor bedroom so she could tramp up and down in comfort when the weather was nasty. Out of doors, ropes and wires that stretched from tree to tree and building to building made a network where she could move about on her own, touching the garden and breathing it in.

Friends came to visit, often for weeks at a time. There were evenings when the dining room filled with the smell of cut flowers, burning beeswax candles, good food, and the French perfume of the women. Helen recognized every guest by the touch of a hand. She knew how tall each one was, so that she held out her own hand at the right height. She was at home, in a place of her own, surrounded by people she loved.

Annie, meanwhile, was puzzling over the riddle of her future. Should she marry John? Did she have the right to when her first duty was to Helen? Even apart from Helen, there was the matter of the considerable differences in ages, as well as her own peculiar moods, her restlessness, and her black depressions. One evening, Annie announced to Helen that she had decided not to marry. "Oh, Teacher," Helen exclaimed, "if you love John, and let him go, I shall feel like a hideous accident!" Annie's mind was made and unmade many times after that; John threatened to print, "Subject to change without notice," at the bottom of the wedding invitations.

They were married at last, and with Helen's whole-hearted blessing. On the afternoon of May 2, 1905, in the flower-filled living room of the house at Wrentham, Dr. Edward Everett Hale performed the ceremony, with Helen standing beside him while a friend translated into her hand.

Then the newlyweds left for a brief honeymoon while Helen went south with Kate.

Several weeks later John, Annie, and Helen were

reunited at Wrentham. It was the start of a new chapter in Helen's book of life, a time "when we three seemed to feel in each other's handclasp a bit of heaven," as she wrote later to John.

They were a family. Although they were tied together in unusual ways, the ties were strong and resilient. John was still Helen's mentor, the older and wiser brother who kept her informed about the chief happenings of the day, political, literary, and scientific. He read to her and went for long walks with her. They played chess together with a set that had been custom-made—the squares of the board cut out so that the pieces stood in them firmly, the white chessmen larger than the black so Helen could see with a touch her opponent's moves. Once, when she was tired, John sat up all night to type forty pages of her manuscript and get them to press on time. When tempers were short—and it happened now and then—it was John who would say, "If we were not a trouble to each other, we could not love as we do."

Snapshots taken during those years show John sitting at a window with Helen opposite, while Annie leans against his shoulder. Helen is slender and erect, with a natural grace. Annie is sturdy, substantial. Both women look affectionately at him, but John looks directly at the camera. In another picture, on the wooden front steps of the Wrentham house, Helen sits beside John and facing him; Annie sits behind him, gazing down at him; and John looks dead-on at the camera. His hair is parted in the middle, and his lower jaw is very slightly thrust forward, very slightly defiant.

The picture captures a characteristic of his, a habit of speaking out and telling uncomfortable truths. As literary editor of *The Nation*, a few years later, he praised James Joyce and D. H. Lawrence, whose books had to be smuggled into the country because of censorship laws. This rebelliousness must have been endearing to Helen; it was a quality she wished for in herself.

About Annie, it was Helen's impression that marriage changed her for the better, that she was less guarded than she used to be. Before, Annie had concealed from Helen her own opinions on controversial matters that stirred her deeply, whether educational, political, social, or religious.

Now, for the first time in eighteen years, they were able to argue as equals. When John read aloud in the evenings, Teacher would spell her comments to Helen. The comments would lead to discussion; discussion would sometimes flare up into a healthy quarrel. Helen believed in women's suffrage, but Annie was scornful of it. Helen's politics were progressive while Annie's were conservative as well as gloomy.

Helen said that the more they talked, the less they thought alike. And it didn't seem to matter. They had reached that stage when mother and daughter recognize themselves as two adults, different in many ways, and entitled to their differences. For Helen, it was the start of a new kind of companionship with Annie.

All three had their separate hopes for the future. Helen hoped for success in writing, or some other field — it was still an open question, the one certainty being that she must earn her own living. John was building a career as a writer and critic; his poetry had already appeared in some of the best literary quarterlies. If he drank too much in those days, it never interfered with work. What Annie hoped and longed for was a pregnancy. She was in her late thirties now, by no means too old to start a family.

Because there were long periods when they had no servant, the women divided the chores between them.

Annie despised housekeeping, but was an excellent cook and gardener. Helen's share was to clear the table, wash the dishes, make the beds, and tidy rooms. These were tasks she had learned to do on her own, and was glad to do, not only because it spared Annie, but also because she enjoyed feeling competent, enjoyed learning every room in the house by touch. She had no sense of direction, and in order to move about on her own she had first to memorize the furniture.

Her heap of correspondence could not be tackled alone. Mostly connected with problems of the blind — mothers struggling with afflicted children, blind young men and women in college, teachers, lawmakers, doctors — the mail, which came from all over the country, as well as England, Germany, and France, had to be read to her in the manual language; she typed out replies by herself.

Now she was working on a book, *The World I Live In*. Apparently nobody cared to read her ideas about the tariff, the conservation of natural resources, or the school system, but they were endlessly fascinated by the life she led in the soundless dark, and this is what she wrote about. One chapter was devoted to smell, another to vibrations; she was extremely sensitive to the harshness of noises like grinding, scraping, and the hoarse creak of rusty locks, while the vibrations of fog whistles were nightmares to her.

In 1907, *Ladies' Home Journal* published an article Helen wrote on an especially touchy aspect of blindness, one that came as a shock to her when she learned about it. The Massachusetts Commission for the Blind, of which Helen was a member, undertook a nationwide census to record the number of blind citizens, where they lived, what ages they were, their cause of blindness, etc. According to this census, much blindness was due to a disease known as *ophthalmia neonatorum* — the blindness of newborn infants. It was contracted when the newborn moved through the birth canal of a mother infected by syphilis.

The disease was easily prevented by a solution of silver nitrate, dropped into the eyes of every infant at birth, a procedure that was simple, cheap, and a legal requirement in France and Germany. America had no such law. And since the words "syphilis" and "venereal disease" were not seen in newspapers at the time, not spoken aloud, certainly not in the presence of women, this meant that American women knew nothing about the cause of blindness in newborn infants.

Helen wrote her *Journal* article with a sense of outrage. She wanted the nation's mothers to demand preventive treatment for every infant at birth: "American women can accomplish almost anything that they set their hearts on, and the mothers of the land together with the physicians can abolish infantile ophthalmia, yes, wipe it out of the civilized world."

It took courage to write those words, since the subject was one of which a young woman was supposed to be ignorant. In Helen's case, it was a question of a very particular young woman, one whom much of the nation had embraced as a miraculous being, transparently innocent and pure. So pure and innocent that some people imagined her mind as a sort of blank slate on which Annie Sullivan had written her own thoughts.

Then, four years after the wedding and five years after Helen and Annie first settled into the farmhouse, the Wrentham household erupted. The image of Helen Keller as innocence personified would be shaken, even wounded, by this eruption. First, John Macy announced that he was joining the Socialist party. Then Helen joined.

thirteen

THE CONVERSION

"This is not a time of gentleness, of timid beginnings. . . . It is a time for loud voiced, open speech and fearless thinking . . . a time of all that is robust and vehement and bold. . . . I love it, for it thrills me and gives me a feeling that I shall face great and terrible things." Helen wrote these stirring phrases for a New York socialist newspaper, the *Call*, and they can be taken as a declaration of how she intended to live the rest of her life.

She made speeches, gave interviews, wrote articles. The language she used in them was outspoken, often reckless. She seemed to be challenging people to see her in a different light now — no longer the student, rising gallantly above her limitations, but part of the active, tumultuous world. She longed to experience danger, preferably in the service of some noble cause, and socialism was the cause she chose, partly because it was an increasingly popular movement. There were other reasons as well.

Vast personal fortunes were typical of the period, one that historians refer to as The Gilded Age. Andrew

Carnegie, the steel magnate, was a prime example. In 1900, his annual income was over twenty-three million dollars — tax-free, since there was no income tax. The average wage of all American workers was then between four hundred and five hundred dollars a year. Most big industries were not yet unionized, and people worked ten hours a day, six days a week. A worker injured in a factory or mine got no compensation from his employer, not even when the injury prevented him from ever working again. In the 1890s there had been about a thousand strikes a year nationwide. In 1904 there were four thousand.

The socialist idea, the one put forward by the recently formed Socialist Party of America, was that competition must be replaced by cooperation, that profit-seeking must give way to social service, and that the result would be a narrowing of the great gap between haves and have-nots. Some socialists were radical, as John Macy was; others, like Helen, were moderate, even conservative.

Helen spoke about her "conversion" to socialism, and explained it as brought about by books that John had lent her. But Helen had never needed converting. Emotionally, she had been a Socialist since adolescence. When she visited the foul-smelling slums of New York, she was reminded of her hopeless and powerless existence as a child. Annie had come to her rescue, and generous friends paid for her education. Surely it was just and fair and right that others should be helped the way she had been helped — factory girls in New York, lumberjacks in the piney woods, railroad workers, coal miners. When they went out on strike, in her mind's eye Helen marched alongside them.

Annie had no interest in socialism. She had no interest either in women's suffrage, feminism, or any system based on the belief that the human race could improve itself. John did his best to change her mind. They argued, sometimes noisily and in public, but Annie refused to be converted. And Helen's conversion was still a personal matter, one the world knew nothing about.

The household had been having money troubles for some time. The fund that supported Helen and Annie at Wrentham came from rich people — capitalists who considered socialism about as desirable as smallpox. This fund had dwindled somewhat since Annie's marriage. The two women knew little about business matters, and all their investments were apparently harebrained. John, whose income was modest, was something of a spendthrift, and Annie worried herself sick about his unpaid bills at St. Botolph, his Boston club. Perhaps they should move to Maine, where living was cheaper.

Then another solution arrived in Helen's mail — an offer of five thousand dollars a year for life, no strings attached. It came from Andrew Carnegie. With his wife, he administered the Carnegie pensions, which helped support men and women who made outstanding contributions to public life.

Helen declined — as a Socialist, she felt she could hardly accept a gift from such a man — but she did it gracefully, charmingly, in a letter that said nothing about socialism. It was only in the winter of 1910, Helen's thirtieth year, that she was ready for a public declaration. She made it in the form of a letter that was sent with a check to the socialist newspaper, *Appeal to Reason*. Fred Warren, the *Appeal's* editor, had been jailed by a federal court for sending "scurrilous, defamatory and threatening" material through the mails.

Helen's letter pointed out that the U.S. Constitution guaranteed freedom of speech and of the press — therefore it didn't take a Socialist to realize it wasn't Mr. Warren, but the federal judges themselves, who ought to be in jail for abridging a constitutional right. "I learn that our physicians are making great progress in the cure and prevention of blindness," she said. "What surgery of politics, what antiseptic of common sense and right thinking shall be applied to cure the blindness of our judges?"

This was the new Helen — denouncing federal courts, including the U.S. Supreme Court — and when the letter was published, her capitalist friends were stunned. So were her mother and Mildred.

Helen hung a large red flag, the symbol of socialism, in the window of her bedroom at Wrentham. She had a reader come in regularly to read to her from the *International Socialist Review*. And in Schenectady, New York, a newly elected socialist mayor — George Lunn, pastor of the First Reformed Church — needed an executive secretary, and offered the post to John Macy.

John accepted. Helen and Annie spoke about following him in the autumn. When this news reached Schenectady it produced unexpected results. The local press announced NOTED BLIND GIRL COMING WITH MACY, with a subhead declaring that the new secretary was going to bring a "famous young woman to Schenectady to live."

Next, the mayor announced the establishment of a Board of Public Welfare; he would appoint Miss Keller to it when she came. Newspapers all over the country then seized upon Helen's forthcoming entrance into politics. They wanted statements, interviews. She told a reporter that her life had only just begun: "All the rest that has gone before has been as nothing. Only the merest preparation — the getting ready to do really great things that shall, perhaps, help all mankind."

Newspaper columns bubbled with Helen Keller and Schenectady throughout the summer. One paper, the antisocialist *Common Cause*, found the subject distasteful: "It would be difficult to imagine anything more pathetic than the present exploitation of poor Helen Keller by the Socialists of Schenectady," it said. And according to the *Brooklyn Eagle*, Helen Keller's mistaken ideas "spring out of the manifest limitations of her development."

With the exception of the *Call*, the attitude of most newspapers to Helen's socialism was equally cruel. She was pitiful, pathetic, limited, exploited by others, they said. Meaning, she was a nonperson. If they expected that she would be crushed into silence by this treatment, they were wrong.

Helen replied to the *Eagle* in a style that was tart and good-humored and very much her own: "Oh, ridiculous *Brooklyn Eagle!* what an ungallant bird it is! . . . When it fights back, let it fight fair. Let it attack my ideas and oppose the aims and arguments of socialism. It is not fair fighting or good argument to remind me and others that I cannot see or hear. I can read. I can read all the socialist books I have time for in English, German, and French."

Because their money problems were still unsolved, Helen had been taking voice lessons again in the hope of doing a lecture tour. The women were less than enthusiastic about Schenectady; even John was restless and dissatisfied there, unsure how long he wanted to stay. Annie, in her mid-forties now, had gained so much weight in recent years that she could only be described as portly. She was moody and depressed, often physically exhausted, and had lost all hope of having a baby.

Suddenly, that September, Annie was taken to St. Vincent's Hospital in Brookline for major surgery. The nature of this surgery is unclear, but for a time there was serious concern for her life — and even when it was clear that she would survive, the Wrentham family was told to expect a long convalescence. John resigned his job to be with his wife; Helen went to friends in Washington, where she wrote to Annie every day and begged for news of home.

She wrote to John as well, asking about the world of labor. Was the Lawrence strike still on? "Please, please don't throw me out of it all, it makes me too homesick." A strike of factory workers in the Massachusetts town of Lawrence had filled newspaper columns worldwide. When the strike leaders were jailed, members of a militant union called the I.W.W., Industrial Workers of the World—otherwise known as Wobblies—stepped in to take their places. They believed in such tactics as boycotts, mass demonstrations, and sabotage. John was an outspoken supporter.

Sometime later — Annie was now convalescing at Wrentham, with Helen at her side — Helen decided that she too was a Wobbly. The I.W.W. had called a strike against knitting mills in Little Falls, New York, and she sent them a check for $87.50, with a letter of encouragement that was read aloud to an enthusiastic strike rally. Even Annie, the least political of people, had been so moved by the Lawrence strike that she too became a Socialist.

Many of the Wobbly leaders were invited to Wrentham, including William "Big Bill" Haywood, the one-eyed firebrand, and Arturo Giovannitti, a handsome young poet. For Helen, having these people in her home was as close as she could get to all that was "robust and vehement and bold." The Wobblies, and the Lawrence strike, had another meaning for her. They had converted Annie to socialism; Annie and John were on the same side now; a barrier between them had vanished, and John could reach out to Annie, embracing her as his comrade and beloved. Or so it seemed to Helen, who had suspected for some time that the marriage was in trouble.

John helped with plans for the lecture tour, the one Helen and her voice coach had been working up to. It was John who chose the first performance hall and decided how much to charge for tickets; the wording of the speeches was also partly his. And in February 1913, Annie and Helen made their first public appearance in the auditorium of a high school in Montclair, New Jersey, with the Montclair branch of the Socialist party as their sponsor.

At least one of her many biographers believes it was also Helen's first public appearance after an operation that replaced her eyes with artificial ones. Until then, she had always insisted on being photographed in profile, because her eyes were uneven in size. But from then on, she would often be photographed full-face.

In any case, it was a very public appearance, and understandably frightening, since she was to stand before people who had paid not only to see her, but to hear her. "Terror invaded my flesh," Helen said later, "my mind froze, my heart stopped beating. . . . Desperately I prayed, as the moment approached to go out before the audience, 'O God, let me pour out my voice freely.' . . . Until my dying day I shall think of that stage as a pillory where I stood cold, riveted, trembling, voiceless."

She survived that first speech and went on to make others. In time, a routine evolved. The first part was Annie's; she spoke for about an hour, telling the story of how she taught the wild creature who was Helen at the age of seven. When it was Helen's turn to go on, someone brought her out to the platform. Placing her fingers on Annie's mouth, she showed the audience the art of lip-reading. Then she gave a short talk, usually a series of inspirational statements full of hope and good counsel. Her voice was never easy to follow; some people described it as high-pitched, with a peculiar metallic ring, but no harder to understand than the speech of a foreigner with a heavy accent. Others called it grotesque.

The next part consisted of questions from the audience: Why was Miss Keller wearing a red dress when she looked so well in white? How could she tell day from night? Which part of her brain did she think with? Was it true she could sing and play the piano and tell when it was going to rain? From start to finish, the performance lasted about two hours.

In April 1913, Helen and Teacher were in Maine for a lecture when the weather turned suddenly cold and Teacher collapsed in their hotel room with flu. Only moments before, Helen had been a confident, capable woman, doing work she was well paid for. Now she was helpless — unable to use the phone because she was deaf, unable to grope her way out of the room because she had never been in it before. Her helplessness was terrifying to her.

Teacher finally pulled herself together and phoned

a doctor. They got to the train station, came home to Wrentham, and within days Helen wrote to Andrew Carnegie, saying she was ready to accept the financial assistance he offered.

His reply was prompt and wonderfully kind. He sent a check that was the first of many, for the Carnegie pension lasted the rest of Helen's life. When John Macy sailed for Europe a month later, his holiday was partly underwritten by one of America's greatest capitalists.

What happened in Maine would happen again, and they knew it. They would have to find a secretary, an aide of some sort, for Teacher's vision was deteriorating, and her general health was not good. They made inquiries but found nobody willing to work as hard as they did. Meanwhile, John wrote to them at Wrentham and they wrote to John, and when he came home at the end of the summer he was drinking heavily.

The women signed a contract with the Pond Lecture Bureau and began a tour of eastern cities. Instead of staying in Wrentham, John found an apartment in Boston; it was one more step in the dismantling of the marriage. Then, in January 1914, Helen, Annie, and Kate set off on their first transcontinental lecture tour, speaking in halls, in big noisy tents full of country people, at a camp on the edge of a lake. Helen kept John informed in letters that were loving and cheerful.

His replies, however, were addressed to Kate, and they were bitter. Annie nagged, he said. Annie tried to influence Helen against him. Annie insisted on centering the life of the household around Helen and was never a wife to him, never did any of the things a woman might be expected to do. Annie "dominated" Helen.

Helen wrote back, imploring him to be "calm, fair, kind." All three of the women went from city to city, hotel to hotel, carrying with them the misery of this dying marriage.

There were other causes for alarm. By August of that year, Europe was at war — Germany and Austro-Hungary against an alliance led by Russia, France, and Great Britain. President Woodrow Wilson urged Americans to remain neutral in thought and deed. But for Helen, neutrality was not possible. How could she remain neutral on the subject of Russia, whose ruler was a tyrant and a murderer of Jews? As for Great Britain, in Helen's opinion that country had built an empire by pushing her conquests to the ends of the earth, "strewing her path with blood, tears and untold crimes."

The European war oppressed her spirits; so did the very real possibility that America would abandon neutrality, becoming a partner with England and Russia in the destruction of civilization. She took these concerns with her when setting out on a second transcontinental tour early in 1915. Luckily for Helen and Annie, they also took with them a new immigrant from Scotland, a young woman named Polly Thomson, who became their assistant, secretary, and loyal friend.

{fourteen}

IN THE THICK OF IT

The lectures were a huge success. Crowds of people came, including Thomas Edison, former President William Howard Taft, and the great tenor Enrico Caruso, who sang to Helen while she "listened" with her fingertips. When she lectured in Detroit, it was Henry Ford himself who escorted her on a tour of his factory.

But when they returned to Wrentham, the house seemed empty without John's presence. Helen longed for him, for the sweetness of family life they had once had, the evenings when he read from the newspaper, explaining the world to her. There was so much she wanted to talk over with him now: ideas, events, and most of all the war.

A British passenger ship, *Lusitania*, was torpedoed off the coast of Ireland by a German submarine; more than a thousand passengers were lost, among them 128 Americans. In the wake of this tragedy, President Wilson's position shifted from neutrality to "preparedness" for war. Although public feeling was actively against Germany, there was no appetite for war, and the country resisted preparedness.

Helen was against both preparedness and war, as John was. Both of them thought that soldiers in the trenches overseas would have to end the war themselves by putting their guns down.

But if their thoughts were parallel, there was hardly any contact between them now. Between Annie and John there was even less, and yet Annie thought of him constantly; her suffering during those days was almost more than Helen could bear. She kept demanding Helen's love in a way that was heartbreaking, Helen said. "For days she would shut herself up almost stunned, trying to think of a plan that would bring John back or weeping as only women who are no longer cherished weep . . . she was too reserved to show her grief openly, and she refused to be comforted. To no one, except myself in the silence of the night, did she speak of her anguish or the terrible dreams that pursued her."

Annie's vision had deteriorated so badly that she could no longer read, and she could no longer take any kind of exercise because of her weight. She was almost fifty and surely facing blindness within the next ten years, a prospect that terrified her. She would not "live blind," she told Helen: She would rather take her own life.

Yet Annie was equally determined that nothing should interfere with the active, useful life Helen was entitled to — a life very much in the spotlight now. In December 1915, Helen agreed to talk about prospects for peace at a meeting sponsored by the Labor Forum. It would take place at Washington Irving High School in New York City, and she let it be known that she intended to advocate a general strike as the surest way to end the European war.

Although local newspapers sent up a howl of protest, an audience of more than two thousand came to hear her. With Annie translating, Helen denounced preparedness as a scheme of the capitalist class for the further enslavement of workers. This brought cheering and wild applause that she felt as vibrations. "Let no working men join this army which Congress is trying to build up" — only munitions makers and bankers like J.P. Morgan had anything to gain from preparedness, she said. More applause. "I hold true patriotism to be the brotherhood and mutual service of all men. The preparedness I believe in is right thinking, efficiency, knowledge, and courage to follow the highest ideals."

When it was over, Helen found an enthusiastic mob waiting for her on the sidewalk, and a police escort ready to take her to her car. Seizing the moment, she delivered another speech right there on the sidewalk. The following day the *New York Herald* wrote: "Nobody can have the heart to criticize poor little Helen Keller for talking when opportunity offers. Talking is to her a newly discovered art, and it matters not if she does talk of things concerning which she knows nothing, could not possibly know anything."

But New York City as a whole — with its sizable immigrant communities, where the socialist faith prevailed — was on fire with enthusiasm for Helen Keller. They wanted another chance to hear her, and the Labor Forum and the Women's Peace Party joined together to hire Carnegie Hall for a second speech. Again she was rash, defiant, and received with wild enthusiasm.

A month later, Helen gave an interview to a reporter from the *New York Tribune*, a woman who noted that Miss Keller was having her nails manicured while they spoke. Anyone who still thought of her as a dis-embodied spirit was about to learn otherwise, the reporter went on — she wore elegant clothes, she insisted on having her nails and hair "done" even for the smallest of small towns, and in spite of her peculiar speech, she said what she wanted to, amazing her friends, her family, and sometimes even her teacher.

"It is here and now," the reporter began, "that Helen Keller, miracle among blind women, makes her debut as an I.W.W." The Socialist party was too "slow", Miss Keller said. It was "sinking in the political bog." This was the reason she had become a Wobbly.

Several friends who were present declared themselves shocked by the statement that Miss Keller was a Wobbly. They implored the reporter not to print it, implored Miss Keller to retract. It would create a sensation, they said; it would ruin her for further peace work.

Miss Keller told them, "I don't give a damn about semi-radicals." She was a fighter now, she said, she would willingly go to jail to uphold her views. In other interviews, Helen described John D. Rockefeller as a "monster of capitalism," while Theodore Roosevelt, a big-game hunter and the nation's leading advocate of intervention in the war, was in her opinion the most bloodthirsty man in the United States.

All this newspaper coverage reached Alabama, where Kate read it and shivered. Her daughter's mindset was entirely different from her own. Although she shared Helen's strong faith in women's suffrage, in other ways Kate was very much a conservative southerner, and the same was true of Mildred, now Mrs. Warren Tyson.

Helen, who understood their feelings, avoided any discussion of politics when she was with them. Kate and Mildred did the same. With sufficient tact on both sides, they managed to keep the family together in spite of their differences. Unfortunately, it was also true that Kate and Mildred saw Helen as set apart from ordinary life. She was more than human perhaps. Or else imperfectly human. If Helen had told them, I am just like you — blind and deaf, but otherwise with the same needs and hopes and emotions as yours, the words would have been meaningless to them. This lack of understanding helps to explain the next chapter in Helen's life.

In the months before it begins, her energies went into the drive for women's votes. She joined the newly formed National Woman's Party, a militant group that was patterned along the same lines as an English suffrage organization, one that had provoked violent police reprisals in the hope of embarrassing Parliament into doing something about women and the vote. "Rights are things that we get when we are strong enough to claim them," Helen wrote in the *Call*.

Then it was summer 1916, and Helen and Teacher started home after a speaking tour. Since Polly was in Scotland with her dying mother, they had engaged a young man named Peter Fagan to act as their secretary. He was twenty-nine years old, a colleague of John's on the *Boston Herald,* and an impassioned Socialist. One newspaper referred to him as slender and fair-haired, but little is known about his background, his habits, his sense of humor or lack of it.

When the travelers came back to Wrentham, they found no sign of John, not even a message to welcome them home. Overcome with loneliness, Helen sent for her mother again. Within days of Kate's arrival, they learned that Annie had pleurisy and a tenacious cough; it looked like the onset of tuberculosis, the disease that had killed her mother and Jimmie.

Their doctor said her best chance for survival was a

sanatorium at Lake Placid, New York. When Polly returned from Scotland it was arranged for her to go to Lake Placid with Teacher, while Helen returned to Alabama in her mother's care. The two Wrentham servants, a houseman and a chauffeur, would have to find work elsewhere.

The household was coming apart. Helen's world was coming apart. Exile in Alabama without Teacher, without the work that gave meaning to her life, amounted to a prison sentence. How long would it last? Suppose Teacher never recovered?

{fifteen}

A LOVE STORY

$\mathcal{M}$ore than most women, Helen was born to love and be loved and to become a loving mother of children. It came close to happening.

The story of what happened instead is told almost entirely by Helen, starting with the day she faced banishment to Alabama and felt overwhelmed by a sense of her own isolation. "Such was the background of the adventure I shall relate. I was sitting alone in my study one evening, utterly despondent. The young man [Peter Fagan] who was still acting as my secretary . . . came in and sat down beside me. For a long time he held my hand in silence, then he began talking to me tenderly. I was surprised that he cared so much about me. There was sweet comfort in his loving words. . . . He was full of plans for my happiness. He said if I would marry him, he would always be near to help me in the difficulties of life. He would be there to read to me, look up material for my books and do as much as he could of the work my teacher had done for me.

"His love was a bright sun that shone upon my helplessness and isolation. The sweetness of being loved enchanted me, and I yielded to an imperious longing to be part of a man's life. For a brief space I danced in and out of the gates of Heaven."

She was eager to tell her mother and Teacher about the wonder of it, but Peter Fagan knew it would not be simple. "Better wait a bit," he said, "we must tell them together. We must try to realize what their feelings will be. Certainly, they will disapprove at first." Her mother had never liked him, possibly because she believed he intensified Helen's radicalism. And Teacher, obsessed by her illness and the loss of John, hardly thought about Peter Fagan at all. He had learned both Braille and the manual language, and their lecture agent considered him a first-class secretary, but in Teacher's opinion he wasn't worth taking seriously.

So there were reasons for waiting. He promised Helen he would win her mother's approval by his devotion; as for Teacher, she was too ill to be excited just now. In the meanwhile, the two young people walked together in the beauty of the autumn woods, and Peter read to Helen a great deal; they must have behaved the way sweethearts behave because both the servants, the houseman and the chauffeur, watched them from a distance and knew they were in love.

The secrecy was troubling to Helen. Teacher would be leaving for Lake Placid in a day or so, and after that it would be too late to tell her. One evening Helen made up her mind to speak to Teacher the next morning.

"But the next morning Fate took matters into her own hands," Helen tells us. She was dressing, full of the excitement of what she had to communicate, and unaware that the *Boston Globe* carried a story about someone called Peter Fagan who had applied for a license to marry Helen Keller.

The bedroom door burst open, and Kate flew in. She held the morning's newspaper with shaking hands, and her movements felt harsh and hostile. "What have you been doing with that creature? The papers are full of a dreadful story about you and him. What does it all mean? Tell me!"

Helen went on brushing her hair, pretending at first not to know what her mother was talking about. "Are you engaged to him? Did you apply for a marriage license?"

Still brushing her hair, still outwardly cool and composed, Helen was terribly frightened. She never says what she was frightened of, or how a mother could prevent a thirty-six-year-old daughter from marrying if she chose to. She knew only that she had to protect Peter, and therefore denied everything. She even lied to Teacher, and did it so well that Teacher believed her.

"My mother ordered the young man out of the house that very day," Helen's account continues. "She would not even let him speak to me, but he wrote me a note in Braille, telling where he would be, and begging me to keep him informed."

In the *Boston Globe:* "Helen Keller and Secretary Vehemently Deny They Are to Wed. Call Story an Outrage." Although Helen had indeed written a denial, she and Peter had made arrangements to meet again.

Teacher and Polly left for Lake Placid. Kate and Helen had been planning to travel by boat to Savannah, then by train to Montgomery, Alabama, where Kate was living with the Tysons. According to headlines in the *Boston Post:* "Helen Keller's Romance Fades, Reported Fiance Quits as Secretary and Goes South, Denying Engagement — May Wed Later, Despite Opposition."

How were they to wed later? It seems that Peter

and Helen had arranged for Peter to board the Savannah-bound boat, and in the interval between the boat and the train the two of them would escape to Florida. A minister friend of his would marry them there.

Somehow Kate found this out in time to change the itinerary. Mother and daughter left Wrentham by train, and traveled all the way south by train. Peter sailed to Savannah alone.

The journey to Alabama must have been heartbreaking for Helen, imagining what might have been, playing over in her mind how close they came to escape, and an end to loneliness. Why had she let it happen? She thought of herself as determined, as a person who knew what she wanted and went after it. Yet she had submitted herself, like a child, to the will of a stubborn mother.

"I cannot account for my behavior," Helen said later. "As I look back and try to understand, I am completely bewildered. I seem to have acted exactly opposite my nature."

In spite of her mother's deception, they were still in touch, still planning for their future. Peter followed Helen to Montgomery. When Mildred saw them together on the porch one morning, talking hand-to-hand, she went upstairs to Kate. Mildred's husband, Warren Tyson, got his gun, and the three of them ran down to the porch. Peter faced the gun courageously, saying he loved Helen and wanted to marry her — but the confrontation ended with his being run off the premises.

Even then, the lovers tried to keep faith. Mildred was awakened in the middle of the night by footsteps on the porch — Helen, having packed her bag, was waiting there for Peter. She waited hour after hour, but he never came. Nobody has ever said why.

Helen came to think of her brief love story as "a little island of joy surrounded by dark waters." Her mother must have thought of it as a lucky escape — but from what? What were her reasons for meddling, for essentially kidnapping the daughter who trusted her?

A possible explanation comes from Mildred's granddaughter, Keller Johnson. She believes that both Kate and Mildred felt there was something "unseemly" about the marriage of a person as severely impaired as Helen. Marriage meant an intimate physical relationship, and they had trouble with that. Her grandmother never said as much, Keller Johnson adds. Yet she gave that impression.

"I am glad that I have had the experience of being loved and desired," Helen wrote. "The fault was not in the loving, but in the circumstances." She was still in Montgomery, virtually imprisoned, with Peter gone from her life, and Annie gone as well — for months, perhaps many months. There was no way of knowing for how long.

Teacher hated every minute of her treatment in the sanatorium. The other patients were old and dull, the weather was hideously cold, and she yearned for escape. Before long she did escape — sailing with Polly for Puerto Rico. It was something done on impulse, on a moment's notice. They found a little cabin in the hills, where for fifteen dollars a month the two of them set up housekeeping. Helen must join them, Kate must join them.

Helen could not bring herself to make such a trip, and she suspected that, in spite of all the sunny letters, Teacher was not doing well. Suppose "something" happened to her? Their financial affairs were tangled; Helen had no idea how to manage them. "If anything should happen to you suddenly," she wrote, "to whom would you wish me to turn for help in business matters?"

Teacher's replies were always reassuring. She mentioned John Macy — "He understands your business better than anyone else. . . . For my own part, I think of him constantly, and since I have been ill much of the bitterness has gone from my thoughts of him. I wish you could forgive and forget too. You would be much happier, if you could, Helen." This was one of the great differences between them, that Annie exploded but then forgave. Helen rarely forgave, especially when someone was unkind to Annie, or ignored her.

In their letters, discussions of money gave way to news. Helen felt almost as far removed from politics as Teacher was. She went for long walks with Mildred, shorter walks with Mildred's two little girls, whom she adored, was entertained by the ladies of Montgomery — and all the while she longed for action. The nation was on the brink of war, but the ladies of Montgomery were not interested in war. Except for Kate, they were not interested in suffrage either. Another topic Helen could not discuss in Montgomery was the treatment of blacks in the South.

She had sent a check for one hundred dollars to the

National Association for the Advancement of Colored People, and with it a letter: "It should bring a blush of shame to the face of every true American to know that ten million of his countrymen are denied the equal protection of the laws. . . . Ashamed in my very soul I behold in my own beloved south-land the tears of those who are oppressed, those who must bring up their sons and daughters in bondage to be servants, because others have their fields and vineyards, and on the side of the oppressor is power. . . ."

The letter appeared in the *Crisis*, a publication of the N.A.A.C.P., and was reprinted by the *Selma Journal*. A number of Helen's relatives lived in Selma, among them Cousin Leila, and they were shocked. So was much of Alabama, including editors of the *Selma Journal* — in an editorial they described her letter as "full of untruths, full of fawning and boot-licking phrases."

Helen kept her thoughts on this subject to herself from then on. But she felt increasingly like an exile, separated from the Woman's Peace Party, and from the radical suffragists of the National Woman's Party. And most painfully of all, from Teacher.

Then, in early April 1917, America entered the war, and Teacher and Polly came home as fast as they could. Helen and Kate went to New York to meet them. "Of course, dear, life will never be just the same again for any of us," Annie had said, months earlier — "it never is after these great changes — we cannot expect it."

The war touched every aspect of life. It clamped down on freedom of speech, on the press, on Helen's comrades among the Wobblies, and on anyone who refused to march in step with militarism. And because the wartime rise in prices had made Wrentham too costly to run, it would have to be sold. Helen wondered how she could bear to part with the place where she, Annie, and John Macy had once been a family.

{sixteen}

"LIGHTS! CAMERA!"

$\mathcal{I}$t was an unpopular war. The government's task was to win the country's support, which might take time, and in the meanwhile to find ways of compelling support. A million soldiers were needed, but in the first six weeks after war was declared only 73,000 volunteered. So Congress voted for a draft.

Two months later, in June 1917, Congress passed the Espionage Act, which would be used to imprison those who spoke or acted against the draft or the war. The post office began taking away the mailing privileges of publications that printed antiwar articles. In Los Angeles, a movie was released that dealt with the American Revolution, and showed British soldiers firing on the colonists' wives and children. The man who made the film was prosecuted for having questioned "the good faith of our ally, Great Britain," and sentenced to ten years in prison.

From Russia, during that eventful year, came news of a socialist revolution in the making. By autumn the Socialists were replaced by the Bolsheviks, but Helen — like many others at the time — saw little difference between Socialists and Bolsheviks. They were revolutionaries; they had overthrown a tyrant; they resembled her I.W.W. comrades, Big Bill Haywood and Arturo the poet, who were sitting in the Cook County jail awaiting trial for offenses under the Espionage Act. Helen said of the Wobblies, "I love them for their needs, their miseries, their endurance and their daring spirit."

She had settled into a red brick cottage on the wrong side of the tracks in Forest Hills, New York, with Teacher and Polly, when a piece of miraculous news came to them. Annie had gone to Lake Placid to be reexamined, and learned she had never had tuberculosis; those first test results had been confused with someone else's.

Now that the sword that had hung over their heads had vanished, they were together again and they expected to live very quietly from then on — three women, their golden Great Dane, Sieglinde, and an old friend from Cambridge days, Ned Holmes, who looked after them.

Early in 1918 their quiet lives were interrupted by an offer to make Helen's life into a movie. A Hollywood movie. Silent, because all movies were silent. The offer came from a man named Francis Trevelyan Miller, who held two advanced degrees and was entitled to be addressed as Dr. Miller.

Dr. Miller explained that the idea for this movie came to him after he read Miss Keller's autobiography and knew that her story must be told to the entire seeing world. Movies were the way to do it, for they spoke a universal language. According to government estimates, in this country alone some 15 million people went to the movies every day.

The women were thrilled, and amazed, and eager to learn more. Not so long before, when Helen graduated from Radcliffe, nobody went to the movies, certainly nobody they knew. Movies were just little bits of things at the time, a jittery travelogue, a fake newsreel, and a vaudeville show, the whole program lasting about half an hour. The "theater" was outdoors, with wooden benches for seats, and people brought newspapers to cover their heads in case of rain; admission was five cents. Now movie-making was the fifth largest industry in America.

Money would have to be raised, perhaps as much as one hundred thousand dollars. And of course Miss Keller would receive "a liberal salary," at the very least fifty thousand. If she had any doubts to begin with, the mention of such a sum would have banished them, for Helen had been troubled for years by the fact that she had done nothing to provide for Annie, in case Annie should survive her. Now there was this opportunity not only to earn a great deal of money, but to carry a message that burned in her heart.

The movie would be called *Deliverance*. A summary of the plot was put together by Dr. Miller. Financial backing was found, a formal contract was drawn up and signed in May 1918. Both women got ten thousand dollars upon signing, and another ten thousand would be paid when the movie was finished. There were royalties still to come.

The next step would be Los Angeles. But before they left, Helen and Annie attended a dinner in honor of the poet Walt Whitman. Helen had been invited to speak. Dr. Miller was there as well, a guest of Helen and Annie, and he heard the speech — in which she deplored the government's persecution of her good friends, the Wobblies.

Panic followed. Dr. Miller told Mrs. Macy she had better explain to Helen that such opinions were dangerous. If Helen continued to express them it was entirely possible that the government, which controlled the railroads under wartime restrictions, might refuse them transportation to Los Angeles. Managers might refuse to let them use theaters. Even if a theater could be found, the public might refuse to look at the picture. In short, Helen had better keep her opinions to herself.

For a while she did. Silence was a price she willingly paid for a chance to bring her message to the public: "As the dungeon of sense in which I once lay was broken by love and faith, so I desire to open wide all the prison-doors of the world." But a few weeks later, Helen was unable to resist joining a group of distinguished educators in a statement to the *New Republic*, demanding a fair trial for the Wobblies. The Justice Department warned the magazine against printing the statement. And Dr. Miller, who was horrified all over again, insisted on a written promise from Helen that she would never behave so indiscreetly in the future.

Helen must have given her promise, however reluctantly, for with Teacher and Polly she set out by train to California, the land where lemon trees grew and where flowers were spread out underfoot like Persian rugs. They met their director, George Platt, a sensitive man with a sound instinct for drama. There was also a Dr. Edwin Leibfreed, whom Helen called "the man who paid the bills." And there were two young actresses, a little girl to play Helen as a child, and another to be Helen at Radcliffe.

Helen played herself in the later scenes, which meant following the director's orders. Annie figured out how to do it. First, she or Polly would spell Platt's instructions into Helen's hand — what she would be doing next, what feelings she was supposed to convey while doing it. A series of taps on the floor would then tell her when to begin a particular sequence of the action — tap, tap, tap, walk toward the window on your right; tap, tap, tap, hold up your hands to the sun.

Helen never felt at ease when acting. She worried about the heat of the studio lights, afraid that her nose and forehead were sweaty; she worried that she couldn't relax, couldn't move easily and comfortably. But she went about her duties as an actress with courage and determination. To George Platt, she was a born trouper, and there were times when he could hardly hold back tears as he tapped out, "Be natural," and Helen tried so bravely to portray her own self for the camera.

Unfortunately, people on the set were beginning to suspect that this part of the story — after childhood and girlhood — offered very little in the way of suspense. Nothing seemed to happen, at least nothing that showed on the screen, because it took place mostly in Helen's head.

Everyone had his own ideas about how to compensate. There was frantic improvisation. Subplots were injected, and strong doses of symbolism. In one of them Helen, the pacifist, was mounted on a large white horse, galloping dangerously forward. While she blew on a brass trumpet, thousands of extras, dressed as shipyard and factory workers, ran behind on the way to *Deliverance*. In another, Knowledge and Ignorance, played by a woman and a man, wrestled for Helen's mind before the Cave of Father Time. Great sums of money were spent on these improvised sequences, with Dr. Leibfreed, the money man, resisting every inch of the way.

They finished filming in December, a month after the armistice that ended the war. Dr. Leibfreed then fired everyone, and hired Dr. Miller back only when he realized the titles still had to be written, which was Miller's job. The unedited film was screened, Teacher and Dr. Leibfreed almost coming to blows about what to leave in and what to take out. Dr. Liebfreed wanted a commercial thriller; Teacher and Helen wanted historical truth.

The women returned to Forest Hills. Since Dr. Leibfreed refused to advance another cent, they had to borrow money from Ned Holmes, the Cambridge friend who lived with them. "I don't remember a time since college days when we were so much 'up against it,'" Helen told her mother. But their credit was good, and everyone waited willingly for their money. As Helen explained to a friend, "There is no doubt of the success of the picture. The big bidders are bidding against each other for it."

Deliverance opened on August 18 at the Lyric Theater on Broadway. According to the *New York Times*, Miss Keller's life was full of marvels, the cast was excellent, the photography exceptionally good, and the film was "one of the triumphs of the motion picture." The *Globe* found it far more compelling than a love story. The *New York World* called it a masterpiece.

After a month or so on Broadway, the rights were sold to a Chicago distributor, who explained some years later that *Deliverance* was appreciated only by "the more refined classes and thinking people, but it did not succeed in drawing crowds to the box office." Nobody made any money on it. Helen and Teacher had nothing more than that first advance, a generous one, but already spent in Hollywood.

The dream of riches evaporated, and with it another dream. Facing her fortieth birthday, Helen saw that the fantasies were over, that what she called her "quaint fancy of leading the people of the world to victory" belonged to her youth and the past.

{seventeen}

ON THE ROAD AGAIN

$\mathcal{I}$n the winter of 1920, Helen started a new career, one that some people considered unsuitable, if not degrading.

She did it for the money, she explained. Another reason was her belief that the blind would be accepted by the world only if they had work — real work, judged by the same standards as everyone else's. Although she never mentioned it, work served yet another purpose: An active mind has little time or energy left for the long thoughts that turn inward, that question fate and the unfairness of life.

What Helen did, in partnership with Annie, was become a vaudeville act.

Lecturing had been dignified, but there were few opportunities left on the lecture circuit. The women had only one story to tell, they had told it, and people didn't want to hear it again. Vaudeville was not dignified. It was acrobats, monkeys, trained seals, tap dancers, horses, parrots, Swiss bell ringers — a grab bag of miscellaneous acts that tumbled across hundreds of stages belonging to the Orpheum or Pantages chains. From coast to coast, in small towns and metropolitan centers, this was the nation's most popular form of entertainment.

Vaudeville came to the house in Forest Hills by way of a young musician, George Lewis, who read the reviews of *Deliverance* and thought Miss Keller might have a chance onstage. He got in touch with a firm of New York theatrical agents and brought them to Forest Hills. It didn't take long for them to agree that Miss Keller would either fill the theaters, or empty them. They were ready to bet she would fill them.

A twenty-minute act was created — a pared-down version of the lecture performance — and thoroughly rehearsed. They opened on February 24, 1920, at the Palace Theater in Manhattan, before an audience as nervous as the actors.

The curtain rose on Teacher seated at a grand piano, a full spotlight flooding her face and upper body. She was in a drawing room, a fireplace with a crackling fire to one side, the piano with a large vase of flowers on it to the other side, and velvet hangings in the background.

Teacher addressed the audience in her soft voice, with its musical Irish brogue. She explained how she came to Tuscumbia and Helen, how Helen went on to Radcliffe, and wrote books, and what her famous friends had to say about her. She quoted Mark Twain: "The two greatest characters in the nineteenth century are Napoleon and Helen Keller." The orchestra played Felix Mendelssohn's "Spring Song," Helen's cue to enter. Polly, waiting behind the velvet curtains with Helen, gave her a nudge. Helen then parted the curtains and walked out.

She was tall, slim, still attractive, and as always elegantly dressed — floor-length dresses with elaborate beadwork were favorites of both Helen and Annie. She shuffled a bit at first when moving along beside the piano. A reporter noted the "troubled hush" in the audience as they watched a blind woman walking about on her own, possibly headed for the edge of the stage with the orchestra pit below. Did she know how close it was? But as soon as Helen reached the piano and the vase of flowers she stopped, lifted her head, sniffed, then buried her face in the flowers.

This was Annie's cue to come forward and lead Helen front and center. Together, they went through the story of the "miracle," the day when Annie spelled w-a-t-e-r into Helen's hand, and the child suddenly knew that everything had a name. They went on to show how Helen had learned speech, and ended with Helen's saying, "Ah-eee ammm nnnot ha-dummm nnnowoo!" "I am not dumb now!" People found that strange, laboring voice tremendously moving.

Then there was a brief question period. Knowing the questions would be much the same as those she got on the lecture circuit, Helen had worked out a list of the likeliest ones and memorized answers. Some were humorous, others sarcastic. There were also times when she said exactly what was on her mind with stunning candor: What did America gain by the war? "The American Legion and a bunch of other troubles." Who are the three greatest men of our time? "Lenin, Edison, and Charlie Chaplin." Do you think any government wants peace? "The policy of governments is to seek peace and pursue war."

"Before she had been on the stage two minutes," the *Tribune* critic wrote the following day, "Helen Keller had conquered again, and the Monday afternoon audience at the Palace, one of the most critical and cynical in the world, was hers." The act was held over for a second week, then went on to Baltimore and Pittsburgh.

There was criticism from friends as well as strangers. Some people wondered how Helen could bear to share a stage with animals and acrobats. Helen's mother, according to Annie, would rather have been "chopped into little bits" than see her daughter in vaudeville. And one old friend assumed Helen never knew about the other acts, that she was being used, manipulated, by unscrupulous people.

If the old friend imagined the manipulating was done by Annie, she was much mistaken, for Annie never liked vaudeville, never adjusted to backstage life with clowns, seals, and tap dancers for company. "She hated the quarrels, jealousies, and pettinesses that are to be found in every profession," Helen said. And she didn't think much of the audiences; they were ordinary, their questions seemed idiotic, and this was not the kind of setting Annie wanted for Helen.

It was also true that the footlights were painful to her eyes, while the noise and the constant rush-rush tore at her nerves. She caught respiratory ailments, laryngitis or bronchitis, one after the other, and was apt to stumble unless Polly walked by her side. A few newspapers commented on how weary she seemed.

Helen, by contrast, was having a wonderful time. "I

Helen Keller reading Eleanor Roosevelt's lips. Mrs. Roosevelt once said in her column that "Miss Keller and my husband typified the triumph over physical handicap." (AFB)

A still taken from the motion picture *Helen Keller in Her Story* showing a delighted Helen with Martha Graham (center) and several dancers (AFB)

Helen lived for a time in Forest Hills, New York. Here, she uses a typewriter at her home there. *(AFB)*

In this scene from the Broadway play *The Miracle Worker*, Anne Bancroft (as Annie Sullivan) and Patty Duke (as Helen Keller) reenact the famous scene from Helen's biography in which Helen first connects the word "water" to the object. (© *Bettmann/CORBIS*)

In celebration of Helen Keller's seventy-fifth birthday on June 27, 1955, the American Foundation for the Blind presented her with a cake. Here, Polly Thomson helps Helen cut the cake. (*AP/Wide World Photos*)

The railings around the house in Westport, Connecticut, allowed Helen Keller to take walks outside on her own. (*AP/Wide World Photos*)

In 1961, Helen Keller and Polly Thomson visited President John F. Kennedy at the White House. (*AFB*)

This photo of Helen Keller's hand on a Braille book was taken in 1933.
(AFB)

Helen Keller reads a book written in Braille, c. 1960 *(AFB)*

Helen Keller writing in longhand *(AFB)*

liked to feel the warm tide of human life pulsing round and round me," she said. "I liked to weep at its sorrows, to be annoyed at its foibles, to laugh at its absurdities." She was welcomed into the workshops where actors kept their costumes and cosmetics. Charming bits of acts were performed for her there, the costumes held up so her hands could examine them. People told her their personal histories, described their heartaches, as well as the "wild parties" they had been to. It meant a great deal to her to be accepted in this way, to belong, to be part of things.

A performer by the name of Will Cressy, who wrote a column for the *New York Star*, left a portrait of Helen Keller during her vaudeville days: "There she sits, in that invisible steel cell of hers, alone in all the universe. And yet, is she as lonely as I think she is? A thousand different expressions are chasing each other over her face. Her head is perched to one side as if she was listening; and yet she cannot hear. Her great big wide-open beautiful eyes are continually shifting around as if she was looking for something; and yet she cannot see. But yet, in some mysterious way, she SENSES many things. Let anyone walk by that she has grown to know, and she learns [to recognize] them as quickly as she does everything else, and she will look up and smile. She recognizes the vibration of their footsteps. If there is dancing going on on the stage . . . she is beating time, smiling, and weaving back and forth and from side to side in time with the music. And always she is smiling. . . . There may be quicker-witted people somewhere in the world than this same Miss Helen Keller, but if there are I have never met them."

While Will Cressy was observing her, Helen observed her audience, but in her own way: "Before I say a word I feel its breath as it comes in little pulsations to my face," she said. She knew when the house was packed, when the audience applauded, laughed, or fell silent. She knew when it was mostly men, because of the strong odor of tobacco. Carpenters smelled of wood, doctors brought the smell of sick rooms and ether, druggists smelled like drugs. They felt protective toward her, just as Will Cressy did, and she must have known that too.

One evening in November of 1921 — they were in Los Angeles, on a second year-long tour — Helen had a telegram from Mildred saying their mother had died. The news came two hours before she was due to go onstage, but she did go on, believing that her private

grief was not the audience's fault. "One of the questions asked me that day was, 'How old are you?' How
old, indeed! I felt as old as time. . . . Another question
was, 'Are you happy?' I swallowed hard and answered:
'Yes, because I have confidence in God.' Then it was
over, and for a little while I could sit alone with my
sorrow." In recent years she and her mother had grown
closer, especially when they traveled together on lecture tours or vaudeville, and this closeness must have
consoled Helen for whatever guilt she felt in needing
Annie more than she needed her mother.

In the winter, soon after their return to Forest Hills,
Helen learned that Dr. Bell had died. One by one, the
people she loved were tiptoeing offstage. She knew
she would meet them all again, "in the Great Beyond
where all truth shines revealed." But there were gaping
blanks left in her life, and some panic when she understood from others how old her teacher looked.

{ eighteen }

ANOTHER NEW CAREER

Christmas Eve, 1923. In Forest Hills a festive dinner was on the table. The guests who gathered to eat it, to sing carols afterward and talk about good works for the blind, included Elizabeth Garrett, the daredevil daughter of a famous daredevil father.

Anyone familiar with the legends of the Wild West will have heard of Pat Garrett, the New Mexico sheriff who brought Billy the Kid to justice. Elizabeth was one of eight Garrett children; blind since infancy, she became an accomplished musician, composer, and public speaker. She also rode horses, bareback and un-accompanied. One day she took it into her head to mount an unbroken pony that belonged to a young deputy sheriff. The pony flew off with her, racing down the road for miles and miles until he wore him-self out, and when he slowed, Elizabeth slipped calmly off his back to sit by the roadside and wait for her fa-ther.

Since then, she had traveled around the country entirely on her own, one of the very few blind people to do so. Elizabeth Garrett was a longtime friend of

Helen's, and living proof that the blind could do almost anything they set their hearts on. Another of the dinner guests, Robert Irwin, had been blinded at the age of five, and went on to become the University of Washington's first blind graduate, later earning a master's degree in education at Harvard.

That evening Mr. Irwin spoke about his appointment as research director of the American Foundation for the Blind, a new organization that would act as a national clearinghouse for the blind. It would decide on the best form of Braille and make it uniform throughout the country. It would build up a supply of Brailled books, discover new fields of employment for the blind, and conduct surveys to learn their needs. The American Foundation had been running on private money since it began in 1921, a few years earlier; now the time had come to create a permanent endowment, with broad public support. Mr. Irwin intended to enlist Helen and Teacher as fund-raisers.

"I confess that I shrank from the prospect," Helen said later. Surely fund-raising was just another word for begging. The blind had been beggars for centuries, holding out cupped hands on street corners because it was believed they could do nothing else. Even though she would be begging on behalf of others, Helen was uncomfortable with the idea.

Annie's feelings were stronger. She had been partly blind as a child, and she knew or suspected that she would be totally blind in old age. This prospect seemed shameful to her, Helen said, as humiliating as a stupid blunder or a deformed limb. But the vaudeville work had fallen away, and idleness never sat well with Helen. Besides, she admired Mr. Irwin, who had succeeded in starting regular day classes for blind children in Cleveland's public school system. She was willing to try. And since Helen was willing, Teacher consented. They would do six months of fund-raising to see how they liked it; during the six months, Helen and Teacher would speak at five meetings a week, in private homes, with the foundation supporting the two of them as well as Polly.

Nobody expected that this tentative beginning would change Helen's life, transforming her into a mover and shaker on the national scene — and internationally, into a representative of America to people all over the globe.

The foundation's president, Moses Charles Migel, who was called Major Migel or the Major, had his reservations about Helen. He wondered about her political views. All her former loves and loyalties and ideals were still in place; if her radicalism flared up again he knew she would be useless to the foundation.

As it happened, Helen realized she could serve the blind best by withdrawing from politics. Besides, the war had effectively killed off the Socialist party, and most of the Wobbly leaders had fled the country. They were still her beloved comrades; she remained a Socialist at heart and was proud to be one, but for the time being she withdrew from politics.

Those first fund-raisers brought the women to several eastern cities, where they were only moderately successful. As Teacher told Major Migel, the old prejudice — that Helen was being used and coached by others — seemed to follow them wherever they went. They moved westward. In Des Moines, Helen spoke before the Iowa state legislature; as the governor later wrote to Major Migel, Helen convinced them "of the importance of doing something for the blind that is permanent and lasting." In Denver, where she addressed the Colorado legislature, lawmakers crowded the floor and packed the galleries to watch her. The foundation began to suspect that whether or not she succeeded at fund-raising, Helen Keller had the makings of a power-ful lobbyist.

Returning to Forest Hills, the women learned that their house had been flooded; there were costly repairs to pay for. New clothing had to be bought; all three descended on the Fifth Avenue shops, and this too had to be paid for. When Annie explained to Major Migel that they needed more money, his response was cool.

Annie flashed back: "I am going to tell you that your treatment of Helen Keller and me does not con-firm the high opinion I had formed of you . . . you bar-gain with us like a railroad magnate employing stokers or road-menders . . . it is a mistake to begin economiz-ing on the driving power of the engine." The engine was Helen.

Major Migel handed the Teacher problem to Mr. Irwin. He himself was busy with preparations for the foundation's 1926 campaign, which would be launched in Washington. President Coolidge was un-able to attend the opening meeting, but he invited Helen and Teacher to call on him the day before, at the White House.

Mr. Coolidge was said to be cold, impersonal, and sour; in the words of Theodore Roosevelt's daughter,

"He was weaned on a pickle." But Helen — a gifted diplomat, and irresistible when she wanted to be — took the president's hand in hers as they were introduced. Then she made some polite remarks, and after a moment's hesitation, said, "They say you are cold, but you are not. You are a dear president."

Mr. Coolidge, with Helen's fingers on his lips to catch his reply, said, "You have a wonderful personality and I am glad to meet you." They went out to the snow-covered lawn and posed for photographers. One of them snapped Helen with her arm around the president. Afterward, Annie talked to the press, and gave verbatim what Helen had said to Mr. Coolidge and what he said to her. "Soon the news was all over the country," she told Major Migel triumphantly.

With the campaign drawing to a close, the Major saw more clearly than ever how deeply the foundation was indebted to them, not so much in dollars and cents, but in publicity, in educational value.

Annie was not comforted by his praise. She told Mr. Irwin that she and Helen could not afford to go on the road again without a raise. Furthermore, they were getting lucrative offers for a lecture tour. There was more correspondence, and several angry threats —

then a most generous offer from the foundation, gracefully worded.

Helen thanked them and declined. She needed at least a year to herself, she said, because Doubleday, which had published *The Story of My Life,* wanted the rest of the story — everything that had happened after Radcliffe. They had been imploring her for years to write it, she had been promising for years to do so, and it was now or never. But if the foundation still needed her after the book was finished, she would willingly take to the road again.

Now Helen turned to a collection of bits and pieces — jottings she had made in Braille over the course of years, articles, letters, odd paragraphs of her own that she had typed rather than Brailled and which she could not read — all of it forming the basic material of the book she meant to write.

She looked it over and thought about it, then thought some more. There were so many interruptions she couldn't seem to get started. Besides, the book would be about herself, and she had had enough of that subject. Most of all, she missed John Macy and his firm editorial hand; since he had left the household, she had published very little. Perhaps she was never cut out to be a writer.

Doubleday silenced her doubts by sending one of its young editorial assistants, Nella Braddy Henney, promising she would be at Helen's service for as long as needed. Nella traveled to Forest Hills every weekday and worked with Helen and Annie for six to eight hours, which would often stretch out to twelve. She learned the manual language and fitted herself almost seamlessly into the Forest Hill circle.

Nella understood from the start how painful it was for Helen to face the subject of this book. The years after Radcliffe were the years of Annie's love story, her marriage, and the tormented death of the marriage. Then there was Helen's own love story, which she was too conscientious to conceal, although putting it into words would mean tearing open an old wound.

Other difficulties had to do with the bits and pieces. Reading the Brailled material was tiring; Helen's arm hurt, the ends of her fingers ached. But material that was not in Braille was even worse, since everything had to be read into her hand; in midsummer, when hands were sweaty, whole sentences melted away. Yet another problem was that Helen could never review what she had written unless it was either put into Braille or read manually to her. Annie was wearing heavy, double-lensed glasses now, and reading was painful for her, so Nella was the only reader. Their progress was tortuously slow.

Still, the day came when Nella was able to carry armfuls of material — notes from her talks with Annie or Helen, letters or clippings from the files — to the Doubleday offices in Garden City, Long Island. She worked up rough drafts of Helen's book, typed them, brought them to Forest Hills, and read them to Helen and Annie.

But this wasn't at all what Helen had expected. It wasn't what she wanted, and it certainly wasn't the way John Macy did things. She explained it to Nella: "Apparently, you thought I would read the manuscript, only changing a word or phrase here and there, and perhaps make suggestions." No, no, not at all, she said. She wanted to write the book as well as she could, and after that Nella was welcome to make suggestions. Helen might or might not agree with the suggestions; what mattered was that the book must be hers, absolutely and entirely hers. Not Nella's.

Nella accepted the criticism, and work continued, but even more slowly now. Day after day, Helen went upstairs to the attic and typed out her life on sheets of yellow paper. Nella and Annie waited downstairs in a little room on the second floor, where Helen would bring the yellow sheets when she finished.

While they waited, the two women talked. They talked about life and love, and whatever else people talk about when they have time on their hands. One of the things they discussed was Annie's life. Privately, Annie had been thinking for some time that she ought to write about it. Friends warned that somebody would — with or without her consent, thus producing a book she would almost certainly despise. Perhaps she should write it now, with Nella's help. The first step would be catching Nella's interest, so Annie began by describing her childhood, the poverty, her father's drinking, and her ruined eyes. The more Annie talked, the more clearly Nella recognized a story almost as dramatic as Helen's, and drew her out.

When Helen's manuscript, "Midstream: My Later Life," was complete, she sent it to the publisher, and Russell Doubleday called it "a noble book." Well received by critics, it enjoyed a solid commercial success.

The year of its publication, 1929, was the year of the stock market crash and the start of the Great Depression. In that same year, Dr. Conrad Berens operated on Teacher's right eye and removed it — there was no other way to relieve the pain. The left eye would require cataract surgery, but Dr. Berens promised to put that off as long as possible, since it would almost certainly leave her sightless. For the time being, he said, what she needed most was rest, a change of scene. When Major Migel came to visit, he helped the women plan a trip to Europe, and told them the foundation was ready to increase their stipend.

Helen talked about Paris, where Teacher would have nothing to do but breathe in the Tuileries, Notre Dame, and Versailles. She would recover some of her old spirit. Even while thinking these thoughts, Helen also knew that Teacher was slipping away from her, from life; she was sliding into despair, and nothing would help.

Annie refused to go to Paris. She moaned and felt sorry for herself and lost her temper, and they had to cancel their transatlantic passage. This made it possible for Helen to go to Washington with Polly. There she testified before Congress on behalf of a bill to appropriate a modest sum, seventy-five thousand dollars, for Braille books for the blind. Support from the federal government for books for the blind — or anything for the blind — was a totally new idea. The bill passed. Then Teacher abruptly changed her mind and the three women left for England, Scotland, and Ireland for a six-month stay.

In the spring of 1931, the foundation prepared to welcome the first international conference of workers for the blind, to be held in New York City. Blind and sighted delegates, with their guides and interpreters, were coming from thirty-two nations, including South Africa, Yugoslavia, Japan, and India. Plans were made for entertainment, school visits, workshops, and discussions of every problem connected with the welfare of millions of blind people worldwide.

Helen helped with fund-raising; she made a speech of welcome to the delegates, gave a reception for them, and flew with them to Washington, to present them to President and Mrs. Hoover. As soon as the conference was over, the Forest Hills trio boarded a steamship for France, bringing with them two trunks, a hatbox, a shoebag, four large suitcases, three small ones, three rugs, three extra coats, and a Scottish terrier named Darky.

The steamship line had found a villa for them in Concarneau, Brittany, with a cook-housekeeper who fed them beautifully and became their friend. But the weather was miserable. Teacher came down with a series of sinus infections that affected her vision. There were hints of cabin fever in the air — until a day in June when the postman brought an invitation from the Yugoslav government. All three women were invited as guests of the kingdom for the purpose of arousing public interest in the welfare of the blind.

It was the first of Helen's many official trips to foreign countries. In each of them she would be received the way state visitors are received. Whenever the cameras captured her she would be surrounded by children and flowers and smiling brilliantly. Part of her charm was this brilliance, this natural glow of a personality that refused to be contained within its steel cell. Wherever Helen went, especially in the less developed countries, she was seen as a symbol of America. Hope and optimism were American, success was American, and these were the themes of Helen's life.

Even her clothing — the small hat with its fluff of dotted veil, the sparkling buckles on her shoes — must have seemed uniquely American, so different from the somber appearance of a blind or otherwise disabled woman in India, or Japan, where Helen visited later.

In Belgrade the travelers were welcomed with music and flowers and a chorus of little Serbian children, all blind and all wearing traditional costume, who sang "The Star-Spangled Banner" for them in English. They were given a banquet on a riverboat; they went to Zagreb, and Bled, and Ljubljana, and on very short notice were summoned by King Alexander to his summer palace. In Nella's account, "the king did what everyone does. He asked Mrs. Macy just how she had taught Helen . . . and Annie Sullivan, child of the Tewksbury almshouse, stood in the royal presence with the grace of a duchess and showed him." "Marvelous! Marvelous!" the king exclaimed.

They were back in Forest Hills by the fall of 1931. When a reporter asked Helen what she had seen in Europe, she told him: "Preparation for war and international hostility everywhere. If the present state of things keeps up in Europe there will be war again within five years."

{nineteen}

THE SAFE FUTURE

*W*ho would take charge of Helen's financial affairs after Annie was gone? She knew she could never bear being managed by Mildred, or by their brother Phillips, and she certainly didn't want to live with either one. What Helen wanted most was to forget about money and investments and go on working for the blind as long as she had the strength.

Annie wanted what Helen wanted. They talked it over with the Major, who came up with a bold and splendid proposal, one based on his conviction that Helen Keller was a national asset. From then on, the foundation would take responsibility for Helen's welfare, which included the welfare of Annie and Polly. So long as Annie lived, she would continue to supervise Helen's affairs; Helen was to choose a committee to act as Annie's advisers, and later as her own advisers. Legal forms were worked up, and in the spring of 1932 the papers were signed by everyone concerned. For Helen and Teacher, the future seemed safe now, as Helen told the Major, and "our life-ship is being steered by wise, trusty hands." She loved him and was deeply grateful to him.

The women were vacationing on the Cornish coast of England that summer, when Helen learned the foundation intended to promote "talking book" recordings and the machines that would play them. Braille books were heavy and ungainly, but with this new system books could be what they were for the sighted, a source of pleasure.

Helen had a poor opinion of talking books, however; to her they seemed frivolous, a waste of money when times were hard for everyone, and especially for those like the blind whose incomes were limited to begin with. "Am unwilling to solicit money for phonographs," she told the Major.

There was another piece of news from home that delighted all three women. For the 1932 presidential election, the Democratic party was probably going to run Franklin Delano Roosevelt. Two years earlier, when he had been governor of New York, Helen had sent F.D.R. one of her fund-raising letters, and an exchange of correspondence followed. "Something tells me you are going to be the next president of the United States," she wrote at one point.

From Cornwall, the travelers moved north to Scotland. Polly's brother, Robert Thomson, had found them an old farmhouse high on a hill in South Arcan, not far from Inverness; it was their hope that the dry air would cure Annie's respiratory ailments. When driving up to the house for the first time, Annie saw a gull near the front door. As she remembered later, the bird "lifted wide wings and flew away over the cornfields." Entering the house, a telegram was put into her hand: John Macy was dead.

"Now my heart is full of withered emotions," Annie wrote, in some notes she jotted down at the time. "My eyes are blinded with unshed tears. Today only the dead seem to be traveling. I wish I was going his way." Although his life and talents had been spoiled by alcoholism, she still thought of John as young, gifted, and intimately her own.

Nella's book, *Anne Sullivan Macy*, was published in the fall of 1933. What began as Annie's life story, to be written with Nella's help, had become entirely Nella's work, a biography rather than an autobiography. The book was a great success, and Helen sent a letter full of praise. But she may have had reservations about it, a secret belief that Nella had not done justice to her subject. Twenty years later, Helen would publish her own biography of Annie Sullivan.

Annie herself had nothing to say about Nella's book. Her world was very small now, bounded on all sides by physical suffering. When reporters questioned Helen about her teacher's health, she wept, and almost broke down. Within a week, Teacher was taken to Doctor's Hospital. She was supposed to rest, and visitors were allowed only a few minutes at a time. "She was worn out," Helen said later, "and, as she confessed to me afterwards, she had let herself drift into futile rebellion against her blindness. 'I have behaved like a naughty child,' she said, 'and cried for the moon and disobeyed all my own injunctions to treat a handicap as an opportunity for courage.'"

They spent the summer in the Catskills, came home to Forest Hills, and then abruptly went to Jamaica, because Annie had been talking about Puerto Rico and sunshine. "The island is beautiful!" Helen wrote to Migel, but Annie went to bed the minute they got there. At home again, she implored Dr. Berens to operate on her remaining eye, putting her arms around his neck and begging him — until at last he did.

By August, they were at home in Forest Hills, where the heat was unbearable, so Helen rented a beach cottage on eastern Long Island, thinking that

Annie could at least take a little exercise and get some sun. One day Annie surprised Helen and Polly by walking down to the water and wading in. Suddenly she grew dizzy and collapsed. The women led her, half carrying her, back to the cottage and put her to bed, as she sobbed, "I am trying so hard to live for you." An ambulance took her to the hospital, where they learned she had suffered a coronary thrombosis.

When the hospital had done all it could, Annie came home to Forest Hills. "In the days that followed," Helen wrote, "it seemed as if my heart would stop beating. Teacher would shift from mood to mood. She would yield to despair. . . . When someone tidied her room, she kept talking to me about the Angel of Death coming for her soon and we should have everything in order at his arrival."

A week later, Teacher drifted into a coma from which she never awoke. Her funeral service was at the Presbyterian Marble Collegiate Church on Madison Avenue in New York City; among the twelve honorary pallbearers, selected and personally invited by Helen, were Major Migel, Robert Irwin, Dr. Berens, and Russell Doubleday. A friend remembered how "all eyes in the church were riveted on the sight of Polly

Thomson and Helen Keller following the coffin together, the tears pouring down Miss Thomson's cheeks. And just as the two of them passed the pew where I sat, I saw the swift, bird-like fluttering of Helen's hands — saw and with a quickened heartbeat knew what I had seen — Helen — think of it — Helen comforting her companion."

Teacher's body was cremated, and the remains placed in the National Cathedral in Washington, the first time a woman had been accorded such an honor on her own merit. Bishop James Freeman presided over the service. "Among the great teachers of all time," he said, "she occupies a commanding and conspicuous place."

{twenty}

WITHOUT TEACHER

*A*fter the funeral, Helen fled to Scotland with Polly, feeling as stupefied as a sleepwalker. The first days on shipboard she had no sense of time, and she ate without knowing what she ate. The fourth day out she wrote in her diary, "What earthly consolation is there for one like me whom fate has denied a husband and the joy of motherhood? At the moment my loneliness seems a void that will always be immense." The thought of work upheld her, religious faith pulled her onward, and Polly stood at her side, a solid and commonsensical presence.

Some of Helen's friends were troubled by Polly's shortcomings. According to Nella, they believed that "Polly would not do. Helen must give up public life, go home to Alabama and live quietly with her sister." Annie, on the other hand, had relied on Polly, who lacked brilliance but was unswervingly loyal.

Polly had doubts about herself. Five years younger than Helen, she was one of four children, two sisters and two brothers, whose father died when Polly was twelve. Their mother did her best to educate the

{196}

boys — but the girls were shortchanged. Polly never married, and her education ended with elementary school. It was Nella's belief that she brought with her "a sense of inferiority from which she never recovered."

In Scotland, now, they were the guests of Polly's brother Robert; with his wife and three sunny children, he rearranged their home to make the women comfortable. There was the usual mountain of mail, largely letters of condolence this time, and Polly read them to Helen just as Annie used to. Or almost the way Annie used to.

One day Polly read letters into Helen's hand for three hours straight, and suddenly Helen understood what the difference was: Teacher had known what to leave out and what to include. "Absentmindedly I made a stupid remark, Polly got nervous, and sharp words flew between us. For several minutes we sat mute with stinging tears in our eyes . . . then we broke down, remembering Teacher's prayer that we might be reunited."

This passage comes from a journal Helen was keeping. A London publisher had proposed a book — brief, simple, only the day's doings with nothing concealed. She wrote about the project to Nella. If the book succeeded, she said, it would be another tribute to Teacher, for then people would see "that I have a personality, not gifted but my own, and that I can stand on my feet socially and economically."

They were still in Scotland with the Thomsons when Helen got a letter from Takeo Iwahashi, whose autobiography, *Light Out of Darkness*, she had very much admired. Blind himself, he had invited her a year earlier to visit his country on behalf of the Japanese blind, but Helen was unable to leave Annie at the time. Now Mr. Iwahashi renewed the invitation. She wrote back, asking for more details.

They went on to London, then Paris, and wherever Helen went she felt the difference between "then" and "now." As she told her journal, "Every hour I long for the thousand bright signals from her vital beautiful hand. That was life!"

But she did not fail to notice preparations for war, forty million gas masks stockpiled for England and Scotland alone. Her German publisher wanted Helen to remove the favorable references to Lenin in *Midstream,* for socialism was frowned on in the new Germany. She refused angrily, and told him to stop publishing her books. The news from Russia was not good — tyranny and purge trials — but the news about German tyranny was worse. Helen still had hope for Russia; one had to keep in mind the misery of that earlier Russia, she said, whose vast peasant population was illiterate and superstitious.

When they came back to Forest Hills, they learned that Major Migel had been in touch with Japan. It was his suggestion that Helen be considered a guest of the Japanese government, and when the Japanese agreed, Migel turned to the White House. Would President Roosevelt be willing to send a message to the people of Japan by way of Helen Keller? It was an exciting prospect.

Helen had always been energized by travel, by tight schedules, meetings, interviews, which helped reassure her that she was not some silent shape hovering at the margins of life. Now, with Teacher gone, she needed reassurance more than ever. The women descended on Henri Bendel's Fifth Avenue shop and got themselves handsomely outfitted. Then Helen turned to her speeches for Japan, sometimes working on them ten hours at a stretch. A long letter from Takeo Iwahashi sounded as if she would be giving six speeches in every city, but even for Helen, "This is a physical impossibility."

On the day of departure, a group of friends came to Grand Central Station to see Helen and Polly off, and when their train reached San Francisco, Helen was given a message from President Roosevelt: "I feel confident that your presence will prove a lasting inspiration to those Japanese laboring under physical handicap, and . . . I take this opportunity to express my hope for the success of your mission." The President's words had been sent, not from the White House, but from Warm Springs, Georgia, where he went for relief from his own physical handicap, the crippled legs that were an aftermath of polio.

On board the ocean liner *Asama-Maru*, Helen got up every day before dawn; while sailors were still swabbing the decks, she walked round and round with Polly, rehearsing speeches. For recreation, she had brought all twelve volumes of *Gone With the Wind*, in Braille, and as she read them, she smelled the South of her childhood, the red earth, the magnolia trees, and her mother's roses. She remembered the demon she was before "that Yankee girl," in the Captain's words, came from Boston to save her.

When the ship docked in Yokahama, they were greeted by thousands of children waving Japanese and American flags. Takeo Iwahashi was there, and representatives of schools for the blind and the deaf, and Joseph Grew, the American ambassador. Grew escorted Helen to a banquet given in Tokyo to honor her, and was astonished by the dignitaries who came to it: the prime minister, the foreign minister, the home minister, the mayor of Tokyo, and Prince Tokugawa, president of the House of Peers. "No foreign visitor had ever been accorded such an enthusiastic reception" said the *Akita Journal*, "not a prince or president, kaiser or king."

What Helen felt was "a loving hand" held out to her, one that lifted her mind above personal suffering. In Tokyo, she was invited to view the cherry blossoms at a party in the imperial gardens, where other guests included princes and princesses, the cabinet, and the diplomatic corps. Helen and Polly were received by the emperor and empress, an exceptional distinction for foreigners.

Japan was hard work. The women went from one end of the island kingdom to the other, with Helen delivering ninety-seven lectures in thirty-nine cities.

Polly believed their visit had already changed the way the Japanese perceived physical handicaps. The old view was the blindness or deafness were visitations of the gods and must be endured with humble patience. But Helen's presence served to demonstrate another attitude: self-help, self-respect, and above all, independence through work.

Helen's *Journal* was published soon after her return from Japan, and reviewers agreed that it showed an alert and lively woman, interested in the real world as well as the world of books, and capable of forming her own opinions. Friends who had wondered whether Helen could manage without her teacher saw that she was indeed managing. With Polly's help, Helen had many good years ahead of her, although she knew — both women knew — that without Teacher, life could never be the same.

In recent years, Helen's work for the blind had been increasingly focused on legislation. With Major Migel and Robert Irwin, she had already succeeded in getting the Pratt-Smeets Bill passed, providing federal funds for the Brailling of books. But when the bill was broadened to help cover the cost of talking books, Helen had balked. She became strident, then furious. Nevertheless, talking books proved to be popular with the blind, and Helen very sensibly changed her mind.

One of her most important contributions concerned the Social Security Act of 1935. This was part of President Roosevelt's New Deal, a broad-based attempt to protect low-income people by changing the rules of the nation's economy. Social Security created unemployment insurance and old-age pensions; there was also federal assistance for dependent children and the disabled. The foundation worked for several years toward inclusion of the blind in the category of disabled, with Helen in the forefront of the fight. She thought the world of Franklin Roosevelt. "The blind of America have cause to bless him," she told Major Migel. "He has done more for their well-being than any other president of the United States."

Roosevelt had a high opinion of Helen. At a Democratic dinner attended by the president several years earlier, the toastmaster mentioned talking books and said Helen Keller was sponsoring them. F.D.R. then passed a slip of paper to the toastmaster, on which he had written, "Anything Helen Keller is for, I am for."

She was well on her way to becoming a national heroine. Polls regularly placed her among America's greatest women, and in years to come, she would be honored by the nation's highest award for civilian achievement, the Presidential Medal of Freedom, conferred by Lyndon B. Johnson.

Now, in 1938, Helen faced a problem that was minor, but pressing. She needed a place to live. The Forest Hills house had been sold because she never liked it. Neither did Polly, and with Annie gone they liked it even less. The women were welcome to stay on until September, the new owner said. But where after that?

On impulse, Helen decided they would go abroad. Incognito. No reporters, no photographers, and her name not to be on the passenger list. Polly would be with her, and Herbert Haas, formerly their neighbor, who had moved in with the women to serve as chauffeur, steward, and man Friday. Haas had learned Braille and was devoted to Helen.

They would go to France, she said. But then it became impossible to think about France. In that same year, 1938, France and England together betrayed Czechoslovakia, surrendering it to Germany's warlords in exchange for a doubtful peace. It was also in 1938 that Germany annexed its neighbor, Austria. An assistant at Vienna's Jewish Institute for the Blind wrote to Helen saying the Nazis had shut down the institute and driven the students out to beg or starve. In the face of such savagery, it seemed to Helen that the only conceivable weapon was a boycott of "the brutal empires," Germany, Italy, and Japan. Stalin's Russia was not included, for she believed that at heart Russia was a peace-loving country.

Meanwhile, construction had begun on a new home for Helen near Westport, Connecticut. Partly supported by the foundation, partly by private philanthropy, it would become a rambling white colonial surrounded by meadows, woods, and brooks. Helen called it Arcan Ridge, after the place in Scotland that was so strongly identified with Teacher.

In the new home she would make new friends, some of them actors, writers, and artists with international reputations. Katherine Cornell, a distinguished actress, became one of Helen's most cherished friends. Others were the sculptor Jo Davidson and his wife, both politically active and leftist in sympathy, and the writer and literary critic Van Wyck Brooks. Helen's new friends entertained back and forth, and took

Helen and Polly to New York for the theater, restaurants, and museums. Helen was almost sixty now, but still young enough to find life exciting.

When the European war broke out in September 1939, she responded the way she had twenty years earlier: "Wholeheartedly I pray that America may stay out of the maelstrom and preserve democracy, its most vital gift to the betrayed, spiritually deaf-blind people." Two years later, the Japanese attack on Pearl Harbor put an end to Helen's affection for Japan, at least for the time being. But Russian victory at Stalingrad — after weeks of street-by-street battles with Nazi troops — was heartwarming to her. She had never stopped believing that Russia would one day create a genuine democracy.

The world would recover from this war, she was profoundly convinced of it. But she also knew that American men were dying in foreign places, and American hospitals were filling up with the war-injured. Although she longed to do something for them, she felt too old, too clumsy and slow-moving. Nella told her to go to them anyway: "You have your two hands, your heart, and your faith in their strength to rise above circumstances."

She knew instantly that Nella was right and asked the foundation for help in arranging visits to the wounded. Once she began, her self-confidence flowered. A soldier asked her, "What gives you the courage to go on?" She told him, "The Bible and poetry and philosophy." And when he said, "How do you feel when God seems to desert you?" she answered, "I never had that feeling." A blind soldier danced with her. The paralyzed tried to embrace her with wasted arms. One young man said, "My, I have not had a kiss like that in years. My mother used to kiss me that way."

With Polly at her side, Helen visited more than seventy hospitals, both army and navy, traveling throughout the South and Midwest and all the way north to Idaho. She called these visits "the crowning experience of my life."

She was very much a public figure at the time, campaigning actively for Franklin Roosevelt — it was his fourth run for the presidency — and her name often appeared in Mrs. Roosevelt's newspaper column. In January 1945, Helen and Polly were invited to a reception for F.D.R.'s inaugural committee. It was a quiet, even sobering affair. The European war was almost over, and it was hard to imagine what would follow — maybe all the old struggles would repeat themselves, the "destitution, rabid nationalism and ignorance," in Helen's words. But she had faith in Roosevelt and his forward-looking courage.

The president died within weeks. As had other presidents before him, he had served as honorary chairman of the American Foundation for the Blind, and Helen presented Mrs. Roosevelt with a resolution that commemorated his service to the organization. Mrs. Roosevelt described her feelings in her column: "As I stood and listened to Miss Keller speak, I thought how wonderfully both Miss Keller and my husband typified the triumph over physical handicap."

With the American Foundation for the Overseas Blind, Helen arranged to visit hospitals for the war-blinded in London and Paris; this was later extended to include Athens and Rome. Writing to Nella just before her departure, she said, "It will mean heartache as I sense over there gusts from the world's distress. . . . But I feel a deep necessity of going."

{ twenty-one }

THE END

*I*n Rome, a transatlantic phone call from the Foundation told Helen and Polly about a devastating fire at Arcan Ridge. The women were stunned, realizing what was lost — letters from their families, Helen's beloved Brailled books, and the partly written manuscript of her biography of Teacher, on which she had worked in spare moments for twenty years. The loss of that manuscript seemed to Helen like a mutilation. But then she remembered the children who were mutilated by fire-bombings in Italy, Greece, and much of Europe, and her own losses became unimportant.

When the travelers returned to Connecticut, they settled into the home of a friend, and before long some of Helen's circle became concerned at what they called her "redness," her radicalism. They suspected it was flaring up again. Robert Irwin believed that Helen's habit of playing around with "Communists or near-Communists" was an embarrassment to her conservative friends, although others encouraged her to stand firm. Each side tugged at her, pouring their arguments into her hand.

But in the summer of 1947, before it became necessary for Helen to choose sides, she was invited to Australia, and within a short time Takeo Iwahashi urgd her to return to Japan. General Douglas MacArthur — under whose steely control American forces occupied conquered Japan — approved of the visit. An around-the-world tour became possible.

Helen hoped for a letter from President Truman, like the one Roosevelt had given her; therefore, she withdrew from every committee tinged with the least bit of "redness," and at the age of sixty-eight prepared to go around the world.

The friends who had been concerned about her political activities were now concerned about Helen's health; she seemed forgetful, not as sharp as she used to be. They worried about Polly too, since she suffered from high blood pressure. Couldn't "the girls" be persuaded to stay home? But of course, once the trip was arranged no earthly power could have kept them home.

The journey began with an uneventful flight to Australia. When the plane landed and passengers were told to debark, Polly saw to it that Helen came down the ramp alone. This meant Polly's taking Helen's hand and placing it firmly on the rail so that she could walk down step by step, light-footed, sure of herself, smiling at all the upturned faces she saw in her mind's eye.

The women toured facilities for the blind in Sydney and Perth, then went on to Canberra to meet the prime minister. Next, New Zealand, then back to Australia after five months of lectures. In a converted bomber, they were flown from Sydney to Japan.

In Tokyo, where Helen spoke before a gathering in the courtyard just outside the walls of the imperial palace, there were said to be three hundred thousand in the crowd. Later, the women were received by the imperial family. Then they set off on a tour of Japanese cities. They went to Hiroshima, the city that was partly destroyed by the world's first atomic bomb, then to Nagasaki, where the second atom bomb was used, "and it too has scorched a deep scar in my soul," Helen wrote to Nella. She promised herself to do everything in her power to fight against atomic weapons.

They had planned to go on to Korea, China, and India. But after Hiroshima, Polly seemed worn out, and an army doctor found her blood pressure dangerously high. After sixty-one days in Japan, the women boarded an army transport at Yokohama and left for the United States.

At the Mayo Clinic in Minneapolis, they learned that Helen was in fine condition, but Polly was not. Nella reported to Herbert Haas, "Polly is exhausted, she is at the breaking point, the danger point . . . she has to live quietly or she won't live at all."

They settled into their new home, a replica of Arcan Ridge built on the same land, paid for by the same generous benefactors. Helen, like Polly, was supposed to live a less hectic life now. Her speech-making was kept to a minimum, although she did a good deal of writing, magazine articles related to travel or to people she knew, with Nella serving as her editor. And she hoped, as everyone in their circle hoped, to find an understudy for Polly.

Then, unexpectedly, in September 1950, Herbert Haas died, and their friends began to worry about the two elderly women living on their own in that over-sized and isolated house. They were further troubled by an invitation Helen had received to make a tour of South Africa.

Of course they went, setting off by ship for Cape Town in February of the following year. Helen had pre-pared herself for a country on the brink of official apartheid by reading Alan Paton's *Cry, the Beloved Country* and Mohandas Gandhi's autobiography. Two years later, they went to Israel, and because the State Department urged it, they visited Egypt, Lebanon, Syria, and Jordan as well. From there they flew to Paris for a ceremony marking the one-hundredth anniversary of the death of Louis Braille. Helen paid tribute to him before an audience at the Sorbonne, in what a friend described as faultlessly grammatical French.

In all their journeys to distant countries, the hardest part was coming home. For weeks they had been treated like royalty, fed like royalty, their wishes whenever possible taken as commands — and afterward they found themselves in a too-large house in Westport, Connecticut, surrounded by several acres of uninhabited countryside. Some of their friends thought they were alone too much. Helen needed stimulation, they said; she was beginning to age, and her remaining senses did not function as well as they used to. On the other hand, a neighbor described her as animated, almost girlish. "When a particularly funny remark is made and handed on to her," he said, "she clicks on the floor in delight, slaps her thigh, and puts her hand over her mouth, depending on how exuberant she feels."

Helen went back to her book about Teacher, the one destroyed in the fire, and Nella came to help her with it. One evening Helen began talking about Teacher's suffering when she first realized that John Macy was leaving. "I thought she would go out of her mind," Helen said, and then burst into anguished sobs. Nella's opinion, as she worked with the manuscript, was that it was written "with passion and insight."

As soon as the book was in the publisher's hands, Helen and Polly prepared for their next long journey, this time to India and Pakistan, and possibly the Philippines. None of their friends or advisers wanted them to go anywhere at this point — certainly not to India, with its heat, poverty, and primitive conditions. But since there was no use protesting, the foundation arranged a big farewell dinner, with Eleanor Roosevelt and ambassadors from the countries on Helen's itinerary. Several people remarked that they had never seen Helen look so exhausted. This time, "the girls" would be gone four months.

The best part of the India trip proved to be the hospitality of Prime Minister Nehru, who invited Helen and Polly for a quiet evening at home with his daughter Indira — "just as if we were members of your family," Helen said, in thanking him. The women toured the country after that, from one end to the other, visiting Gandhi's tomb and the Taj Mahal. Brailled page proofs for her biography of Annie — she gave it the title *Teacher* — came by air express, and Helen was able to proofread them.

They were back at Arcan Ridge by June. A week before Helen's seventy-fifth birthday, she went to Cambridge for the Harvard commencement ceremonies, at which she was awarded an honorary degree, the first Harvard ever gave to a woman. One observer said of Helen, "She never looked more beautiful — all in white with a white dress with tiny green flowers on it."

Her birthday was marked by telegrams and gifts from all over the world, and six months later, *Teacher* came out in time for Christmas. It went fairly well at first, but within a year the book had slipped from sight. Nella noted in her journal that one of the drawbacks was Helen's style, "rather ornate and dated."

Now a new literary work entered her life. The playwright William Gibson sent Nella the script for a television drama based on Teacher's letters as they appeared in Helen's first autobiography. Gibson called it *The Miracle Worker.* When he came to New York and met Nella, almost the first thing he said was, "You can see that I am enamored of Annie Sullivan." In Nella's opinion, the script had both dramatic power and literary merit, but Helen never cared for it, and Polly liked it even less.

On a day when Helen and Polly were alone at Arcan Ridge, they were visited by the disaster everyone had been dreading. Polly, who was fixing lunch, suddenly began to sway. She had trouble breathing, and said she wanted to go out to the terrace, but it was so cold outside that Helen persuaded her to come in. Polly went back to fixing lunch, turning on the burners of the electric stove. Helen, hovering over the stove in a state of controlled panic, immediately turned each of the burners off.

Polly's legs began to buckle, and Helen led her to the bathroom. Polly tried again to fix lunch. . . . Two and a half hours after the start of Polly's heart attack, the postman saw the open terrace door and phoned for help.

Afterward, two nurses were found to care for Polly, and the foundation sent a secretary to handle Helen's mail. Friends who came to visit found the place gloomy; Helen said she was old and tired, and wanted only to be left alone. But the television production of *The Miracle Worker* was such a huge success that Gibson was determined to bring it to Broadway, perhaps even make a movie after that.

Nella explained to Helen that *The Miracle Worker* was going to bring in a great deal of money, especially if it became a movie. According to their arrangement with Gibson, Helen and Nella would receive 20 percent of whatever he got. The money was to be shared between them, half to Nella for *Anne Sullivan Macy,* half to Helen for *The Story of My Life.* All the details would be handled by Nella, who had Helen's power of attorney.

Nella soon learned that where a great deal of money was concerned, there was bound to be discord. The first hint of trouble pitted Nella against Helen's advisors, the foundation trustees. There were letters back and forth, questioning the power of attorney Nella had been given in 1948. Then *The Miracle Worker* opened on Broadway, a smashing success from the start. Not long afterward, Helen sent Nella a note that had been signed by witnesses: she was canceling the power of attorney. Nella, who was deeply wounded, tried to understand what had happened. She came to believe it was somehow connected with Polly's hostility to *The Miracle Worker* and Polly's jealousy of the role Annie had played in Helen's life. It could just as well have been Helen who was jealous, who could no longer bear the thought of sharing her teacher with anyone, not even Nella, although Nella had been for so many years her own devoted friend.

Even Helen's trustees seemed to understand that the loss of Nella left Helen unimaginably lonely. When Polly Thomson died in March of 1961, Helen's loneliness deepened — yet her spirit tried, as always, to rise above self-pity. In a letter to Robert Thomson, Polly's brother in Scotland, Helen wrote, "Now I sit by her empty chair thinking of the fidelity with which she helped me in my difficult work and the tireless cheer with which she took part in our amazing adventures. I am sure that now they have met in Heaven, Teacher is prouder of Polly than ever."

Nella wondered who would dress Helen now, who would rehearse her speeches, and stand beside her on the platform as interpreter. But there were no more speeches, no public appearances. With Winifred

Corbally, one of the nurses who had cared for Polly, Helen lived quietly at Arcan Ridge. In Mrs. Corbally's eyes Miss Helen was beautiful, and great fun, and happier than she had ever been.

A year after Polly's death, Helen suffered a mild stroke that was followed by several more. Five years later, Mrs. Corbally wrote to Phillips Keller, saying of Miss Helen, "My poor darling is walking that last mile so very slowly."

Helen had been thinking about the last mile for a great many years. The subject came in the spring of 1950, during a pleasant luncheon at the home of Margot Keller de Besozzi, a distant cousin who lived in a seaside village in Italy. Helen and Polly had stopped there on the way to Florence.

They would be seeing Michelangelo's famous statue of David, Helen said. "I'm so thrilled. I've always wanted to see it."

One of the guests turned to Polly in amazement. How could Helen hope to see the "David"? As Polly explained, "The Italian government has had a scaffolding erected around the statue so that Helen can climb up and touch it. That's what she calls 'seeing.'"

Then the guest asked Helen — by way of Polly — what else she intended to see in the course of the trip, and Helen answered for herself. Her diction was not normal, the guest noted. She spoke haltingly, "like someone who has had a stroke, and her consonants were slow and labored. She turned to me, looking directly at me because she had sensed where I was sitting." Helen carefully mapped out the journey, naming the places she meant to visit and the people she would meet. "There's still so much I'd like to see," she said, "so much to learn. And death is just around the corner. Not that that worries me. On the contrary."

"Do you believe in life after death?" the guest inquired.

"Most certainly. It is no more than passing from one room into another."

They sat in silence for a few moments. Then, slowly and quite distinctly this time, Helen spoke again: "But there's a difference for me, you know. Because in that other — room — I shall be able to see."

In June 1968, when she was eighty-seven years old, Helen Keller succumbed to heart disease and entered the other room. She was cremated according to her wishes, and her ashes brought to the National Cathedral in Washington. The choir of the Perkins School sang at the service, then the urn that held Helen's remains was placed beside the one that held her teacher's. According to one report of her death, the attending physician noted a smile on Miss Keller's lips.

{bibliography}

ALLEN, FREDERICK LEWIS. *The Big Change.* New York: Harper & Bros., 1952.

BROOKS, VAN WYCK. *Helen Keller, Sketch for a Portrait.* New York: E.P. Dutton, 1956.

BRADDY, NELLA. *Anne Sullivan Macy.* Garden City, New York: Doubleday, 1933.

BRUCE, ROBERT. *Alexander Graham Bell and the Conquest of Solitude.* Boston: Little, Brown, 1973.

FONER, PHILIP. *Helen Keller, Her Socialist Years.* New York: International Publishers, 1967.

GREENBERG, JOANNE. *Of Such Small Differences.* New York: Holt, 1988.

KELLER, HELEN. *Helen Keller's Journal.* Garden City, New York: Doubleday, 1938.

KELLER, HELEN. *Midstream: My Later Life.* New York: Greenwood, 1968.

KELLER, HELEN. *Out of the Dark.* Garden City, New York: Doubleday, Page, 1913.

KELLER, HELEN. *The Story of My Life.* Garden City, New York: Doubleday, 1954.

KELLER, HELEN. *Teacher.* Garden City, New York: Doubleday, 1955.

KELLER, HELEN. *The World I Live In.* New York: The Century Co., 1908.

LASH, JOSEPH. *Helen and Teacher.* New York: Dell Publishing, 1980.

PALMER, LILLI. *Change Lobsters, and Dance.* New York: Macmillan, 1975.

REPPLIER, AGNES. *Agnes Irwin, a Biography.* Garden City, New York: Doubleday, Doran, 1934.

ST. GEORGE, JUDITH. *Dear Dr. Bell — your friend, Helen Keller.* New York: Putnam, 1988.

THARP, LOUISE HALL. *Adventurous Alliance.* Boston: Little, Brown, 1959.

ZINN, HOWARD. *A People's History of the United States.* New York: Harper & Row, 1980.

{acknowledgments}

Grateful thanks for advice and never-ending patience to Kenneth Stuckey, curator of the Samuel P. Hayes Library at the Perkins School for the Blind.

The Perkins School for the Blind, in Watertown, Massachusetts, has an extensive collection of material related to Helen Keller, including letters, journals, and papers of Anne Sullivan; Nella Braddy's papers; and news clippings.

{ index }